CORPORATE
CHARACTERS

Other Books by David A. Bragen

A Beginner's Guide to a Successful Career

ForeWord Magazine awarded a Gold Medal in the career category to *A Beginner's Guide to a Successful Career* in 2005 as part of its sixth annual Book of the Year Awards program.

From a letter to David A. Bragen from Susan Driscoll, president and CEO of iUniverse:

"This year's competition yielded a record-breaking number of 1,500 entries; A Beginner's Guide to a Successful Career *looks like a wonderfully practical guide for those entering the work force (in fact, I'm ordering one for my son!) and I'm delighted that it has now been recognized as one of the finest independently published books of 2004."*

A Beginner's Guide to a Successful Career is available online at Amazon.com and Booksamillion.com.

CORPORATE
CHARACTERS

Understanding the Personalities
of
Your Co-Workers

DAVID A. BRAGEN

Award-winning author of *A Beginner's Guide to a Successful Career*

iUniverse, Inc.
New York Lincoln Shanghai

Corporate Characters
Understanding the Personalities of Your Co-Workers

Copyright © 2006 by David A. Bragen

iUniverse books may be ordered through booksellers or by contacting:

iUniverse
2021 Pine Lake Road, Suite 100
Lincoln, NE 68512
www.iuniverse.com
1-800-Authors (1-800-288-4677)

ISBN-13: 978-0-595-40910-5 (pbk)
ISBN-13: 978-0-595-85272-7 (ebk)
ISBN-10: 0-595-40910-5 (pbk)
ISBN-10: 0-595-85272-6 (ebk)

Printed in the United States of America

CONTENTS

To Kent and Larry for helping me cope with the transition from employee to business owner. Thanks guys. It would have been a lot more difficult without your counsel and constructive criticism.

To my wife Sharon for standing by me all those years when my employment took me away from you and the family. Sorry for the missed birthdays and anniversaries.

To my children Richard and Susan for having to grow up with only a part-time dad. I should have been there more.

And to Rachel and Jan at iUniverse for helping make this a better book.

PREFACE

Every journey starts with a first step.

The first book I wrote, *A Beginner's Guide to a Successful Career*, is presented in a conversational style. I personally find this style not only easier to read, but, as an author, much easier to write. It's easiest to express our thoughts through a casual, but meaningful, conversation. Therefore, it is the style I have used for this book as well.

Regarding language, the editor who worked with the original manuscript of *A Beginner's Guide to a Successful Career* suggested that I not use any off-color language—not that I had used much of it in the first place. I followed his suggestion and rewrote several minor sections. In this book I follow that same sage advice, though, as I reminisce about some of the characters I've come across in my corporate career, some very colorful— or maybe that's off-color—language comes to mind!

I'm assuming there are equal numbers of men and women reading this book. And all the characters discussed in this book—from the best to the worst—appear in life in equal numbers of men and women. So, to avoid the awkward use of "he or she" throughout this book, and in the interest of equality for all, I have arbitrarily assigned one or the other gender in my examples throughout.

Last, though I may describe some of the Corporate Characters with passion, either positively or negatively, I do my best to describe personality types as opposed to specific people. Any similarity to any particular individual is unintended.

So, with these caveats in place, let us proceed by introducing ourselves to a number of Corporate Characters.

INTRODUCTION

November 11, 2005, marked my 32nd anniversary in business. During those thirty-two years, I experienced quite a few highs and lows. And though the number of highs clearly outweighed the number of lows, the lows were truly devastating, both to my family and to me.

The highs included starting my first job; receiving compliments on my performance; getting raises and promotions; changing career paths; opening up a new sales office in my territory and moving my family to a new house; signing a major contract with an important customer; becoming an elected officer of the company; changing companies and achieving even higher levels of authority, responsibility, accountability, and compensation; and starting my own business.

The lows included getting yelled at; not getting a raise on time; being passed over for promotion; getting demoted; leaving my first-choice company; losing a major account; getting fired; and starting my own business, which eventually turned into a high.

The companies I worked for and the industry in which I plied my craft are really unimportant to this story. They were big companies; in fact, at one time, each was able to lay claim to the fact that it was the world's largest in its industry. The industry was huge, and even the small segment in which I actively participated totaled well over a billion dollars of revenue every year.

Throughout the course of my career I came into direct and indirect contact with thousands of people. In my own business now, even though I am essentially working in the same industry I always worked in, I am encountering many new people. The differences are that I am now dealing with different parts of those various organizations, and, at my age, I am finding that many of my old contacts are retiring, or are being phased out by some other means and being replaced by the next generation.

The vast majority of the people I have come into contact with throughout my career are typically decent, pleasant, and hard working. Like me, they work because they have bills to pay, and would probably prefer to be doing something else if it weren't for those financial responsibilities. Yet, despite the need to work, most of them have decided to face their situations positively and to focus on turning their jobs into careers. They feel as if they are making a contribution and are part of a team. And, while it might be a stretch to say they like to go to work each day, they do take pride in their efforts and they do try to do a good job.

During my thirty plus years in business, life in corporate America has shifted from what, in many cases, used to be a cradle-to-grave environment to one in which uncertainty is the watchword of the day. People no longer work for only one company throughout their careers. In fact, most résumés nowadays catalog multiple previous employers, especially since downsizing, right-sizing, and plain old fashioned cutting back have become the boogiemen waiting outside the door.

People used to be able to sharpen their skills and move up the ladder if they wanted to. And if they didn't move up within one company, they moved over to another that would pay for their experience, rewarding them with raises and promotions just to "come join us." Now, experienced people are very often the first to be let go—not because of poor performance or lack of effort on their part, but because they are simply the people that are being paid the most. And when the business must reduce expenses, the size of the target on an employee's back is in direct proportion to the size of his paycheck, unless, of course, he's one of the few who are making the decisions as to who should be let go.

As executives began to feel the need to make sure that they could cash out on their stock options, it changed the way these executives looked at those under their care: greed became the motivator for many of them, or, in some cases, caused them to become sloppy and lazy in the way they approached managing their people. People really became their most important asset—an asset that was both saleable and expendable. And, while I don't believe many executives consciously plan on cheating their minions, the lure of the big bucks does jade their view of the world. So they can wreak havoc on people's lives, and then they can find solace in collecting their bonuses and stock options in return. And when the stock price goes up, even though the service levels of the company go down, they're hailed as the outstanding leaders of business. And, like a rat leaving a sinking ship, they dance to the tune of the executive headhunter and jump from one company to another, lured by the promises of even higher bonuses and even better stock options.

But let us get back on task.

Corporate Characters is a book that presents and dissects many of the personality types that you will encounter during your career. And even if you don't yet have or want to have a career, and are only working at a job because you really, really need the money, having insight into why some people do what they do is always helpful.

Borrowing an idea from the title of a Clint Eastwood film, ***The Good, the Bad and the Ugly***, this book is sectioned into a triad of personality types and will enable you to categorize almost every individual you will ever meet throughout your working years. Some of these people, **The Good**, will become fast friends and colleagues—people you truly enjoy interacting with during the work-a-day world in which we live. Others, **The Bad**, are people you will put up with because they're there and you simply have to work with them. You will limit your involvement with them and even actively seek ways to avoid them. And the last group, **The Ugly**, are those SOBs who truly seem to go out of their way to make your life, and the lives of many, miserable.

THE GOOD

People you will really want to get to know

The Co-Worker Who Starts
on the Same Day

After receiving my BBA in marketing from Loyola University in Chicago, I applied for a full-time position in customer service at the same company my father worked for—a company where I had spent two previous summers working in the manufacturing end of the process to help defray the costs of college. My first interview went well and I was scheduled for a second. This particular company was noted for hiring family members of existing employees, so I had high hopes of getting an offer. Two days before that second interview, one of their largest customers announced that they were going out of business. The impact was devastating on both my dad's company and me. Overnight, several hundred people lost their jobs when a dedicated manufacturing plant, designed specifically for that customer's product, was shut down. And an immediate freeze was placed on all outside hiring as the company scrambled to find alternate positions for some of the affected employees.

I had vicariously grown up with the company through my dad and my summer jobs and was disappointed that I did not get the job I was interviewing for. Instead of looking elsewhere for employment, I decided to return to Loyola for an MBA. Nine months into the MBA program, I received a call from the corporate recruiter at my dad's company, who informed me that they were looking for an estimator, and wondered whether I'd be interested. I said, "Yes!" I then proceeded through three more interviews and was finally offered the position, which started on November 11, 1974. I worked full time and continued to attend the MBA program part time at night, finally getting my advanced degree in 1977.

On the first day of my new job, I reported to my new supervisor (we will hear more about him in another section of the book), who told me to go to the medical department for my "company physical."

As I entered the medical department, a nurse who must have been in her early sixties greeted me. Later, when the doctor emerged from his office, I noticed that he too looked like he was nearing retirement. Now I have nothing against older people, especially since I'm knocking on that door myself, but at the tender age of twenty-two my first thought was, "Thank God I'm not really sick! This place looks like the inside of some dungeon laboratory out of a Lon Chaney horror movie, and these two look like Lon's parents!"

The nurse handed me a clipboard that held several health and insurance forms, and told me to sit down and fill them out …"and print neatly!" I sat down next to a middle-aged factory worker who had a paper towel wrapped around a finger that was dripping blood, and a factory worker in his mid-twenties who was bent over in the chair, holding his head in both hands. He smelled like a brewery. Between the blood and the stale beer smell, I decide it was a good time to move across the room to another row of chairs. Just after I sat down for the second time, the door to the office area opened and in walked an attractive young lady, about the same age as I. She walked up to the nurse, said a few words that I could not hear, and was handed a clipboard and given the same set of instructions I had received …"and print neatly!"

She walked over to the two rows of facing chairs and was immediately confronted with a decision: deal with the blood and the beer smell on the right side or the lecherous grin of a recently graduated young man on the left. Talk about a tough decision.

Casting her fate to the wind, she decided to sit down on my side. Who knows why? Maybe it was the tie. She smiled a quick hello and dove into filling out the forms. After a few minutes we started talking about a couple of the questions that were ambiguously worded, quickly established that this was our mutual first day on the job, and filled each other in on our backgrounds. Jennifer (not her real name) and I became good friends—a relationship that lasted throughout my fifteen years at that first company.

Now, the category of The Co-Worker Who Starts on the Same Day really encompasses a wide mix of people, some of whom you will meet in other first-time situations. It may be someone you meet during a training seminar or on a visit to a customer's office. It may be an employee in another department, or even the person sitting next to you on an airplane.

These kinds of encounters are non-threatening interactions that happen when any two people are thrown together in a circumstance that encourages a verbal interaction. People tend to speak to each other in these cases and, since the encounter is almost accidental, each understands that the other party is not a threat: no one wants anything particular out of the interaction. There is no hidden business or personal agenda. It is simply a case of two ships passing in the night. And with the threat of a predetermined need for some form of specific outcome being non-existent, both parties in the interaction can let down the barriers and simply be who they are.

What makes these encounters interesting is the fact that, without the perceived threat that accompanies many first business meetings between two people, we are able to allow each other to examine our real selves. If one or the other has a sense of humor, it will quickly show. You will easily share your thoughts and opinions, all of which are taken at face value. And, while you may not agree with everything that is said to you, and may even enter into a spirited debate on some issues, both of you follow the unwritten rules of engagement that allow for this type of interaction. Yet, if we cloud that same conversation with expectations we have of people we are meeting and interacting with for specific business reasons, we become judgmental in our thinking, assessing and analyzing every comment and statement made to us, looking for hidden agendas and unspoken meanings.

I'm sure you encountered these situations before in your every day life.

It's amazing how much information people will share with a total stranger. You may tell the person sitting next to you on the airplane all of your personal troubles and she may share the same with you—typically things you wouldn't tell your neighbor or even a close friend. And you do this because the interaction is purely non-threatening to each of you. You are kindred spirits who have found themselves in the same situation, at the same time.

Because of these circumstances—almost accidental meetings—people tend to be themselves and not establish the artificial barriers people sub-consciously erect when they sense the need to protect themselves from the unknowns. Since I know the person sitting next to me on the airplane has no expectations of me, does not have any preplanned reason to talk to me, and is simply talking to me to kill time (assuming he chooses to speak and I choose to respond), I feel relaxed enough to be myself and escape for a short period of time into a safe, non-threatening world. So, before you know it, you and the person next to you—whether on the plane, in a seminar, or at the counter of a crowded Starbucks—have established the basis for friendship. Sometimes these friendships develop into longer-term relationships with the exchange of business cards or telephone numbers. More often, though, they become the once-and-done interactions that make us think, "Nice guy" or "Nice gal" as we walk away, never to meet again.

The basic premise here is that most people—probably close to 80 per-cent of people in my humble opinion—are decent. You may not com-pletely like 80 percent, or want all of them to become members of your intimate circle of friends, but you don't dislike them. And these people form a large part of your daily contacts. This group of people may include the guard at the front door of your office building, with whom you share a quick quip on your way into work every morning, the guy from the mailroom who drops off your correspondence each day, the person sit-ting next to you in a training seminar, or the assistant of the buyer you're meeting in a sales call.

This network of contacts will grow over time as you simply encounter more and more people throughout your career.

And the biggest benefit of these encounters is that you will get to know these people, albeit on a somewhat superficial level, as they really are. They won't be hiding behind the barriers that normally get erected. They are not out to impress you, sell you something, or make a request of you—or vice versa. They are simply there to exchange a brief greeting or a nod of recognition. Or, the conversations can become longer. You may exchange more ideas and thoughts until you actually start to seek out each other's company because you want to spend more time together. Hello friendship!

This informal, almost accidental, network often blossoms into more meaningful individual relationships that can have a positive impact on your career. For example, the executive assistant at your customer's office—the one with whom you always shared a smile and a nice word—gets a promotion and becomes an assistant buyer. Or, the person you spent time with in the medical department that first day of work turns out to be someone you need to work directly with in the future.

In these situations, where interactions are not forced and no obvious or hidden agendas exist, people tend to exhibit the following characteristics:

- They are pleasant in their style of conversation.

- They are open about their feelings.

- They are considerate to you.

- They can debate a point with you without making their expression of difference feel like a personal attack.

- They seem open to new ideas and are ready to share their opinions as well.

- They have similar interests; yet also add potential new opportunities in terms of expanding your experience base.

- They have no expectations in terms of trying to get something out of you, other than momentary companionship.

- In simple terms, they are nice.

Looking back at this brief list of attributes, you could argue that what I have described is what people typically refer to as a friend. Surely friends that you have known for a long time exhibit some other characteristics as well, but I submit that if you don't see these basic characteristics in a new acquaintance, your relationship probably won't develop into a friendship. People tend to gravitate toward people they like, and relationships flourish into friendships as individuals discover more and more about one another. Identifying common ground is an important foundation upon which friendships can and will develop.

The following diagram demonstrates the difference between acquaintances and friends:

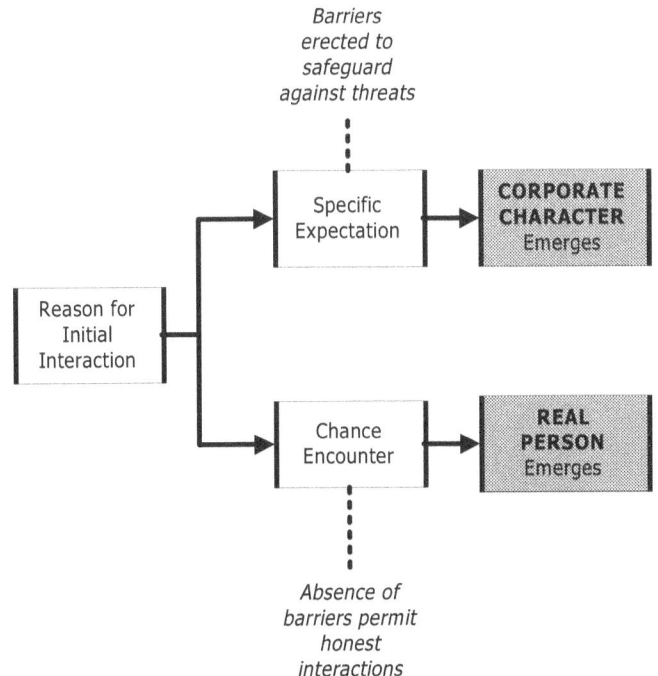

As we said previously, we all experience a number of these first-time, almost accidental meetings with people. These are just a couple more examples in addition to those already mentioned. There are business luncheons for charities, where you might find yourself at a table with representatives from another company or a governmental organization. You might attend a charity round of golf sponsored by your company where you find yourself with three people who may be complete strangers, and usually, by the time you finish the round five hours later, you all have a good understanding of one another and may want to add one another to your informal networks.

And while we are on the subject of networks, which will also be discussed in several other sections of this book, let us introduce the subject here and lay some groundwork.

"Network" and "networking" are a couple of words that are thrown around frequently. There are those who simply define a network as a person's list of names and telephone numbers. There are others who suggest that a network is made up only of your most intimate contacts. In between these two extremes is a vast range of the various levels of networks that exist. We will just concentrate on two of them: the formal network and the informal network.

Formal Network

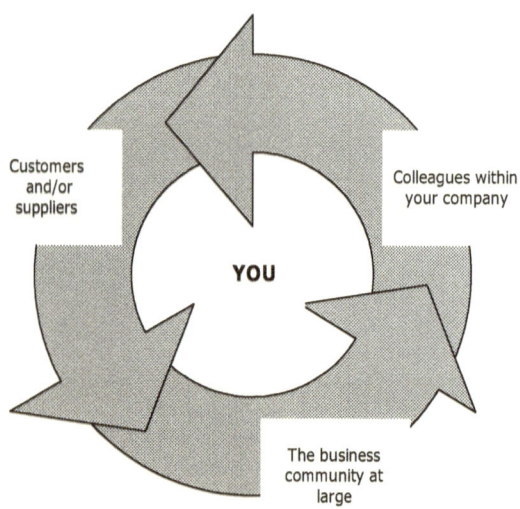

The formal network that we develop throughout the course of our business career is made up of three distinct elements: colleagues at work, customers and suppliers, and the business community at large.

Your colleagues who work at your company are an important segment of your formal network. These individuals, in theory at least, are on the same team as you are, have the same goals, and work together for the greater good of the organization. Of course, this isn't always true. Some co-workers will never be colleagues and not everyone is interested in the same goals, or even the common good for that matter. But, in general, colleagues at work are an important part of your formal network.

Then, we have customers and suppliers. These individuals come into your life because of their needs and wants, or because their goods and services have a direct impact on whether or not you will be successful in the long run. These people become an integral part of your daily corporate life—either directly because you are in sales or purchasing or manufacturing, or indirectly because, without them, your company would not need you as an accountant, a raw material tester, or a general manager.

And, finally, we have the business community at large. These people may be competitors, prospective suppliers or customers, members of another company serving the same industry your company serves, or people you meet through other business activities undertaken by your company.

The common thread running throughout a typical formal network is the very fact that it is formal. It exists as a means to an end. It serves to benefit all members of the network and, because of this, your individual success or failure is linked, at least to some degree, to the actions or inactions of the other members of the network. You network with your customers in order to make more sales. You network with your suppliers to increase the quality of their raw materials, to reduce their costs, to gather industry information, and, at times, to seek assistance in finding a job. You network with the business community at large to improve their perception of both you and your company, or, to fulfill the role of being a good corporate citizen. But whatever the reason, you have developed and have become part of a network that has the understood, but unwritten, mission of providing benefit to the various members.

Now just because someone is part of a formal network does not necessarily mean that he will actively participate and follow the rules of engagement. Some members of the formal network do not want to be members of the network. These reluctant members are members just because of the position they hold. For example, the president of your company's largest customer—the account that you just happen to be assigned to as the sales person—is a network member. She realizes that without your company providing her company with the products or services they buy from you, her life would be more difficult. On the other end of the spectrum, your management expects you, as the sales person on their largest account, to have solid relationships throughout the customer's organization, up to and including their president. You go to a cocktail party sponsored by your company and, lo and behold, there, across the crowded room, you see the president of your largest customer. You quickly slip into the networking mode, scurry over to her side, say, "Hello," and strike up a conversation—any conversation. The president, grateful that you remembered to reintroduce yourself, puts on her cocktail party mask, smiles and says, **"Of course I remember you, Joe. How are things going at ABC Company?"** After several comments and questions fly back and forth, you notice that the president's eyes are scanning the crowd in search of an excuse to end the conversation. Being a savvy sales person, you recognize the signs and allow her a graceful exit.

Back at the office the next morning, when your boss asks you about the cocktail party, you regale him with a lengthy recap of the short conversation you had with the president of your company's largest customer, making sure to convey the fact that the president is a member, albeit at arm's length, of your formal network. At the same time, the president of that company is talking with someone from her company, recalling the fact that once again "The sales person from ABC Company ... I never can remember his name—John? Jason? Whatever. He practically ran across the room just to say hello. What an idiot!"

Clearly, this is a harsh appraisal of the formal network. Or, is it? Every formal network is not a waste of time. Nor is every member of a formal network dragged in, kicking and screaming, protesting their "forced" membership. Yet many members are members simply because of the position they hold. And there will be those few people who simply refuse to become part of your formal network.

Building a formal network can be equated to the sales process. You need to give someone a reason to want to become a member of your formal network. Just because you want him to become a member, especially an acknowledged member, will not make it so.

Informal Network

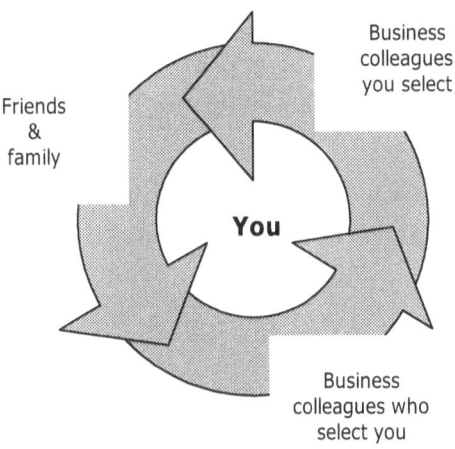

Your informal network is a clean slate until you start to add its members. Unlike a formal network, where membership to some degree is pre-determined, an informal network provides you with complete freedom of choice as to who should and should not belong. And since the informal network consists of people who have openly or tacitly agreed to become members, the network evolves as an end, and not as a means to an end.

The distinction here is important to understand.

The formal network comes with a predetermined list of members and exists to accomplish specific goals and tasks: Sell more products and services. Get a better deal. Look for a better job.

The informal network is a by-invitation-only club that exists to provide its members with open, unbiased, and candid support and advice. The informal network is your ad hoc self-improvement committee where you will seek counsel and provide counsel. Its purpose is to provide for the betterment of each and every member. Each member has an equal share. At one time a member may be the person who is being asked to give. At another time that same member will be the person who is asking to receive.

The people we meet through accidental circumstances—the person starting the job on the same day you do, the other members the foursome in a charity event golf outing, the person sitting next to you on the airplane—are prime candidates for your informal network. So are members of your family, some special colleagues at work, and your intimate circle of friends. Not everyone is a candidate, nor is every candidate worthy, so choose wisely.

A separate section of this book deals with networks, so suffice it to say, we have laid the groundwork at this point for the future development of this topic.

Let us return to Jennifer for a while.

After we received our company physicals, which really amounted to little more than filling out forms, getting our blood pressure checked, and having our pulse taken, Jennifer and I walked over to the human resources department together to get our employee manuals, get our pictures taken for the ID cards, and fill out the tax forms. In total, we had spent the better part of the morning together and, since it was close to lunchtime, we decided to go to the cafeteria together.

By the end of lunch, we felt that we knew each other and felt comfortable with one other. We tacitly agreed to become friends though we worked in different departments. Sometimes we'd go weeks without seeing each other while, at other times, we'd run into each other two or three times a day. When time permitted, we always took a few minutes to catch up on what was happening in our personal and business lives. We knew we could trust each other and that what we said would remain in confidence. We learned from each other and each became for the other an informal information source for what was going on in other parts of the company. And we looked out for each other, pointing out opportunities and warning of potential pitfalls.

Our relationship was not based on the need to achieve certain outcomes. It was not based on a business necessity. We were not members of a formal network. We were the first two members of a new, informal network at the company that we both started working for on the same day, when we met in the medical department to get our company physicals.

The Friend

When I returned to the estimating department after lunch, my new supervisor, about whom we will hear more later, asked me to come into his office. We spent the next few hours reviewing departmental policies and procedures. Then he walked me around and introduced me to the other supervisors, all of the estimators, the administrative assistant, and, finally, the department manager. People greeted me with various levels of enthusiasm, or lack thereof. Some seemed genuinely happy to meet me; others seemed bothered by the trouble of having to associate yet another name to another face, while the balance demonstrated the passive acceptance of someone who couldn't care less that a new person was starting.

Before I knew it, the first day had ended and I met my dad in the parking lot. I still lived at home at that point and we drove to and from the office together. Naturally he was curious about my impressions and all that had transpired during my first day. I guess my descriptions were somewhat unimpressive for, after a few minutes, he reached over, turned on the radio and said, "Tomorrow will probably be better."

The nature of my position required that I needed not only to be trained to be an estimator, but also in the entire manufacturing process so I could, in fact, estimate jobs. The estimator's job was to take a request for a quotation from the sales force, develop a plan of manufacture, identify the costs associated with producing the job per that plan, add markups for profit, draft the proposal language, obtain the required price level approvals, and forward all information to the sales person who would actually turn the information into a formal customer quotation. Long story short: training lasted approximately three months.

One of the training sessions I was scheduled to attend included a week-long stay in one of the manufacturing plants, which was approximately 200 miles south of my hometown of Chicago. The day before I left, I was informed by my supervisor that a senior estimator from another section, someone I knew well enough only to say hi to in the morning, would accompany me on the trip since he had a project to work on with others at the manufacturing plant. The plan was for my trip partner, let us call him Ralph, to meet me in front of the corporate building and for us to take his car to the facility.

Ralph worked in an area called expansion planning. The function of these highly trained and skilled estimators was to evaluate plant and equipment expansion opportunities. When the sales force uncovered an opportunity so large that it exceeded existing capabilities and capacities, it was Ralph's job to identify what equipment was needed to produce the work, then locate a piece of property in an appropriate state, contact the local government to inquire about tax breaks and other governmental assistance, build the plant from a financial perspective, and help sales identify a price for the customer that would be both salable to them and profitable for us.

To those of us who didn't personally know Ralph, our impression was mixed. Clearly, his talents were obvious. He was smart, had experience, was well spoken in both oral and written communications, and commanded the respect of his peers. On the other hand, he was at times loud and boisterous, acting like a prima donna. So it was with a little trepidation that I embarked on this weeklong trip with the semi-stranger named Ralph.

The conversation during the first thirty minutes of our trip was filled with details of our backgrounds. I found out that, while we were far from being twins, we did have quite a few similarities. Soon the conversation turned to work-related topics—not assignment-specific topics, but more of the water cooler, office-gossip type of topics. Before I knew it, he had me laughing so hard I was crying as he told me stories and rumors about this person or that. I began to see Ralph as a totally different person. Here we were, experiencing an almost accidental interaction, and we were both acting like the people we really were, with no false pretenses about professionalism or our relationship as colleagues working at the same company … just two guys on a road trip.

Over the course of that week, Ralph and I truly bonded. We had breakfast together, rode to the plant together, and though we worked separately during the day, we met after hours for the ride back to the hotel. We'd end the day with dinner, a few beers, and quite a few more laughs. Then next morning, we'd do it all over again. By the time we were driving back to Chicago, we were planning on meeting for dinner at his house so I could meet his wife. I was single at the time and it became their mission to find me an unattached female.

Ralph and I became close friends and confidants. In fact, he stood up at my wedding. We helped each other throughout our careers, even when assignments caused us to go our separate ways for a while. We were always only a telephone call away. Ralph became the second member of my informal network.

The Friendship Model

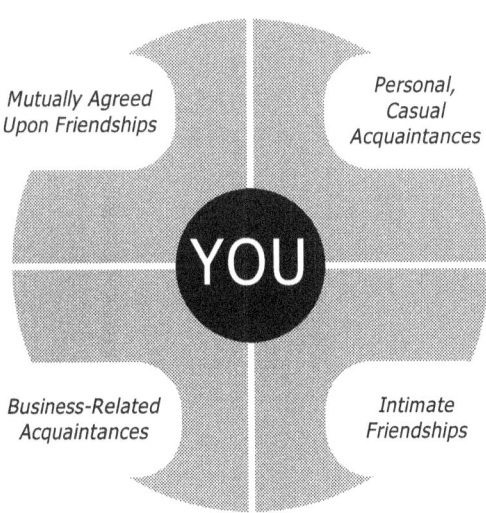

Mutually Agreed
Upon Friendships

Personal,
Casual
Acquaintances

YOU

Business-Related
Acquaintances

Intimate
Friendships

Obviously, not everyone you meet or come into contact with will become a friend. In fact, most of the people you come into contact with will fall into one of two categories: either they will become casual personal or business acquaintances, or they will simply not become a part of your life. And while a lot of people claim to have many friends, we really need to peel back the layers to see whether or not those friendships are solid, intimate, and true friendships, or simply casual friendships born out of convenience or necessity.

For example, let us look at the person occupying the office, cubicle, or desk next to yours. Let us say you consider him a friend. Heck, you talk to each other just about every day, have coffee together, meet for lunch occasionally, help each other on projects, commiserate over the loss suffered by the city's NFL franchise, ask what the other did this past weekend, and inquire about the health of his family. Like I said, you are friends, but at what level?

Looking at the model above, we can argue that this must be a mutually agreed upon friendship. While it's personal and casual, that description suggests a non-work environment, something you may have with a neighbor or the parents of the kid who is on the same Little League team as your child.

It is a fair assumption that the only two reasons that you know the person next to you at work are that you work for the same company and occupy space in close proximity to each other. So, let us agree that the relationship you have with the person sitting next to you in the office is a business-related acquaintanceship. The relationship is certainly more than just a morning head nod acknowledgement, but definitely not a close, intimate, personal friendship.

So what? Maybe John or Jane in the next cubicle over is only a business-related acquaintance. What's the point? The point is that for the good of your own career and peace of mind, you need to know the differences in the levels of friendship that exist between you and others. You also need to know where the various people you come into contact with reside in the "friendship model," also keeping in mind that many people do not even appear in the model.

Expanded Friendship Model

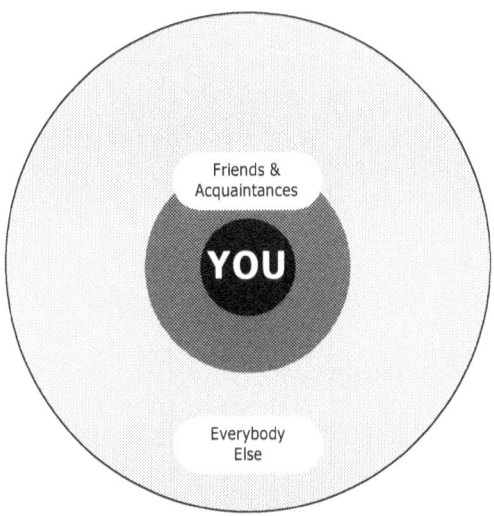

The old adage tells us that a friend in need is a friend indeed. And, if your need is a simple ("Would you please pass the salt?"), anyone can be a friend. But when the need is a serious, career-impacting situation, you'd be surprised at how many of your friends at work will treat you like yesterday's news. So, understanding the various levels of friendship and knowing where your friends reside on that scale is very important. Important because you don't want to be surprised when the person you ask for help all of a sudden acts as if he doesn't even know you, or is too busy, or offers any one of a hundred excuses why he cannot accommodate your request. When real needs arise, you need real friends to help you.

Of course, to have true friends, you need to be a true friend yourself. The street does run in both directions. So, treat people as you expect them to treat you, and remember that you will reap what you sow. Unexpected acts of kindness lead to unexpected acts of kindness in return.

Let us explore the specific characteristics that correspond to the four levels of friendship on the previously introduced model:

Mutually Agreed Upon Friendships

- Common, personal interests form the basis for both the initial attraction and future expansion of the relationship.

- Though both parties may not have started out on a mission to find a new friend, both were subconsciously positioned to follow this course of action should sufficient reasons develop for continued pursuit.

- Friends are willing to help and assist each other, but typically establish boundaries beyond which they will not venture.

Personal, Casual Acquaintances

- A relationship typically develops because of the situational dynamics that surround the initial contact.

- Boundaries are established quickly in terms of topics discussed and emotions shared.

- Both parties typically understand, accept, and adhere to informal rules regarding requests for help and assistance.

Business-Related Acquaintances

- Common business interests form the basis for the initial attraction, though future expansion of the relationship may be based on either business or personal interests.

- Both parties inherently understand that, except for the necessity of the business needs, the developing relationship probably would not have started in the first place.

- As the business need for the relationship declines and eventually ceases to exist, so will most of the relationships formed under these circumstances.

Intimate Friendships

- There is an absence of quid pro quo accounting for favors and good deeds requested and provided.

- Boundaries are relaxed or non-existent for topics of conversation and emotions shared.

- Both parties understand that they can reveal themselves entirely to the other party and not be judged.

Your Friendship Filter

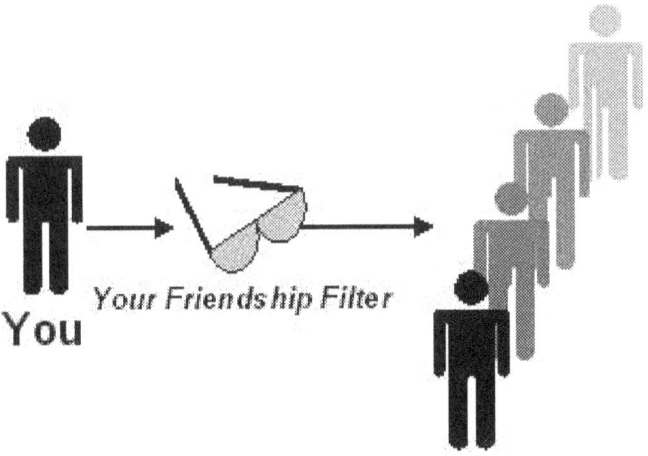

Though you rarely choose the people with whom you have to work, you can and do decide who will and will not become friends. However, we must also recognize that each of the other members of our work family has the free choice to seek and develop us as a friend as well.

Each of us is a unique individual, shaped by our genetic makeup and upbringing as well as by environmental dynamics beyond our control. We are products of our environment, which unfortunately allows people we meet for the first time to develop stereotypical mental images of us before they get to know the real person that we are.

He was a jock in college, therefore he must be a bit slow in the mental department. She went to that East Coast university, so she must be smart. He came from the south side of town, therefore his family must be well off. It happens all the time to most of us, and we do make snap decisions about others in our own mind.

Then, to confuse the process further, we have to factor in first impressions. Exhibit a good first impression and people have a positive feeling toward you. Stumble and you provide someone with the opportunity to form a negative first impression of you, forcing you to struggle through a some-times long, tedious process to change that initial negative impression.

We will talk about teams in another section. For now, we will concentrate only on those people whom you will seek out, or who will seek you out, in hopes of developing a friendship.

People typically like people who are somewhat like themselves. If I like something and you like the same thing, we've identified one topic around which we may decide to develop a relationship, or we at least have achieved a jumping-off point for exploring an expanded relationship. And when enough commonalities are uncovered, we feel we have found a kindred spirit and start spending more time together. We have lunch together, share a coffee break, or volunteer to work on the same project.

These relationships are rather easygoing and happen quite naturally as you, the new person, try to fit into the group dynamic while your co-workers try to determine whether you are future friendship material.

The foundation upon which a friendship is based varies from person to person. The following model is meant simply to suggest that, as more similarities are identified, the basis upon which future relationships can be established becomes stronger.

Key Interest Model

Your Network

During your career, you will come into contact with many new people. Some of them will become good friends, while most of them will simply be people you work with. There will, however, be a select few that become members of your network, and herein exists one of the fallacies regarding networking that many people don't understand until it's too late. You may want someone to be part of your network, and by outside appearance she is a willing participant, but many network members become network members only for their own benefit. Or worse, they give the appearance of being a member, but really are not.

The unwritten rules of networking provide for give-and-take relationships between the willing participants. I may contact you to ask a question, solicit aid, or request an opinion. I expect that you will respond by either giving me the information I seek or by telling me you are unable to help but suggesting another avenue I could take to get help. Correspondingly, as a member of a network, I should expect my telephone to ring or to receive an e-mail from some other member making the same kinds of requests of me. This is the give-and-take aspect of networking.

In some cases, however, people who appear to be willing and active participants of the network are there simply for their own benefit. They are not concerned with your well-being and will provide only enough assistance or information to remain in the loop. Or, they won't have any answers or the ability/desire to assist you and are unable to suggest any alternative sources. Yet, when they are in need, they will hound you relentlessly.

Networks are not meant to be a substitute for good old-fashioned hard work. You are still expected to solve your own problems and identify your own opportunities. But having access to a network will assist you in formulating those solutions and will help you uncover and identify opportunities.

Business-oriented networks are helpful in many areas:

- They act as sounding boards for idea development.

- They serve as information sources.

- They provide a forum for problem solving.

- They provide opportunities for introductions and door openers.

- They provide some semblance of emotional stability during trying times.

- They act as safety valves to enable members to blow off steam without compromising their careers.

Business-Oriented Networking Model

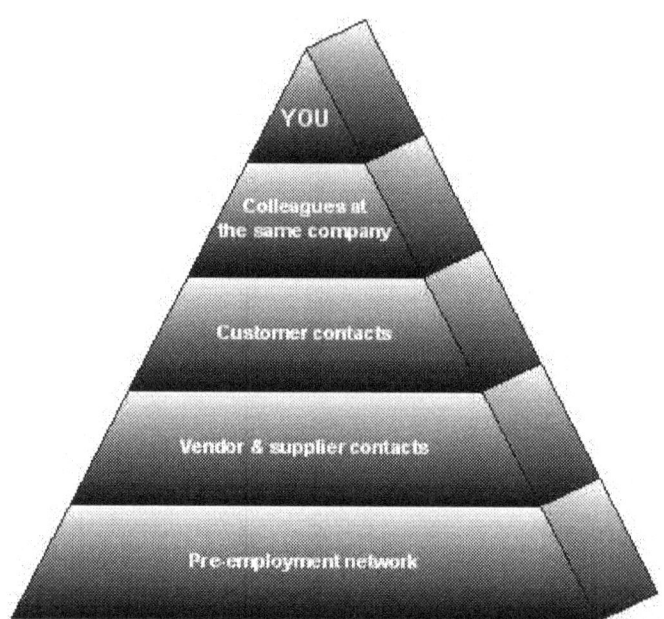

Representative Network Hierarchy

The purposes of a network are many and will vary among each person and situation. You may even have several networks, depending upon their purpose. You might have one that is comprised of creative individuals who can assist you in developing plans and strategies. You may have another network that is made up of seasoned professionals who can come to your aid in times of difficulty. And you may have the all-important contact network, which acts as a safety net when you find yourself in need of a new job. But your first network will usually be an ad hoc committee of people you meet within the first few months after you start a new job in either a new company or in a new department.

You will come to find that Frank is the guy that everyone runs to with a difficult question regarding market pricing. Or, Mary is the recognized expert when it comes to developing sales strategies. Or, Bill in the shipping department knows everything there is to know about trans-Atlantic logistics. Who ever these people are, and wherever they may reside in the organization, they will form the backbone of your network.

As time goes on, you will add people to this expanding network who do not work for the same company you do. They will be suppliers, or customers, or someone from your previous interactions. Over time, you will treat your network like a baseball team, trading out some members, and searching for new members with special skills and experiences. While Bill in shipping may remain in the network, he cannot answer the questions concerning the legal aspects of the warranty clause your customer is demanding so, like a scout for the New York Yankees, you have to keep your eyes open for additional talent.

And, as they do in baseball, once you have identified a potential network member, you give him a tryout. Is he approachable? Is he willing to help? Is his advice and counsel productive and accurate? Is he willing to become a member of your network?

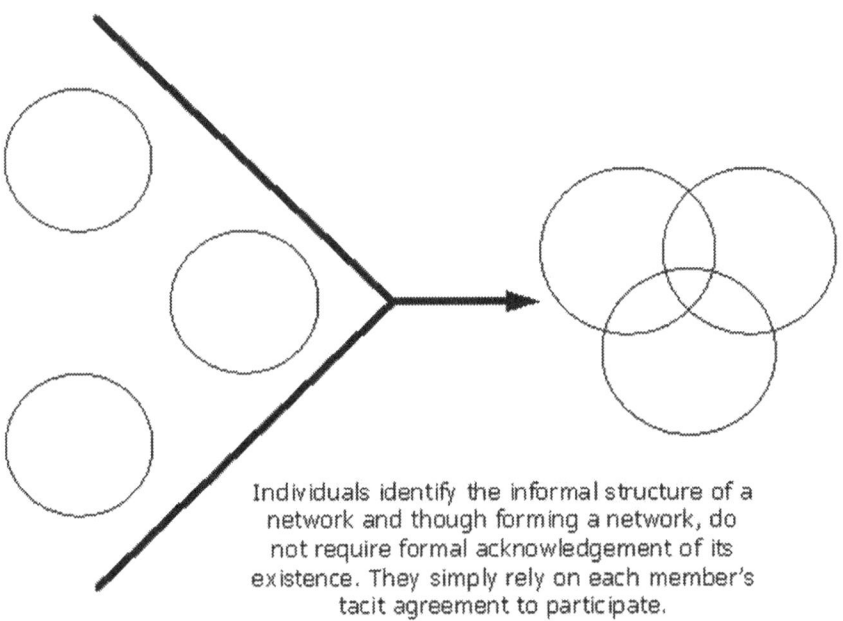

Individuals identify the informal structure of a network and though forming a network, do not require formal acknowledgement of its existence. They simply rely on each member's tacit agreement to participate.

Networks tend to develop informally. There really are not any membership questionnaires to fill out or interviews to go through, yet both parties typically engage in conversations that suggest a willingness to develop an informal relationship or, on the other hand, they may send signals indicating that they'd rather not participate.

As you progress during your career, and as you move into different assignments with different levels of responsibility and authority, your status in these informal networks will change. At one point you are the new member who naturally takes more than you give. You then graduate to become a mid-level member in which the give-and-take typically balances out. And, quite probably if you continue in the network, you end up a senior member, where your capacity for giving far outweighs your need for taking.

The people who populate your network will generally do their best to assist you wherever they can. They won't do your work for you or make the decisions that are yours to make, but they will provide insights and opinions that you will need to carefully consider before you do embark upon a course of action. You have formed your network and populated it with these hand-selected people because you value their contributions. You have most likely built into the network a series of checks and balances to make certain you uncover a number of options when faced with any problem or opportunity. So, Bill the optimist balances Mary the pessimist. Susan the extrovert balances Steve the introvert. Rich the technician balances Sharon the artist. And at the end of the exercise, you will have been exposed to a series of insights, opinions, thoughts, and ideas that will enable you to sculpt the solution to fit the problem you face, or to develop a strategy to successfully achieve the task at hand. Your network will serve its purpose and help position you for success. And when it's your turn to be the contributing member to another member's challenge or opportunity, you will return the favor.

The Smart One

Throughout my career, I have had the opportunity to work with some truly intelligent people. I'm talking about people who really have high IQs, are creative, are quick, are experienced, and are more interested in successfully completing the task at hand than in making sure they are singled out for their contributions. Companies need people like this, because many times these people form the backbone for successful sales, projects, departments, product lines, manufacturing plants, and the like.

These individuals are gifted, yet human. They have an enormous capacity to soak up information like a sponge, remember it, and, most importantly, combine it in ways that help them overcome the highest hurdles in their path—or in your path if they're part of your network.

And since they're human, they also have the same character flaws that most of us possess in one form or another. Of the four smartest people I've happened to work closely with during my career, one was a drunk, one was socially inept, one was a borderline schizophrenic, and the last was a political time bomb. Yet, I called each of these people friends at the time. They were my friends, and I was their friend in return. They helped me many times in many ways and I tried to return the favor to whatever degree I could. And, in one case, just being a friend was help enough.

The Smart Ones are like the
information signs along the
journey that becomes your
career. Miss them, and the
trip is a lot less interesting.

The smart one is an almost self-contained, one-person network. She knows so much about so much that having her on your side is so much better than not having her—or worse, finding out that your competition has someone like her on their side.

But, you must beware of and understand just who the smarts ones really are!

Throughout your career, you come across the fast-trackers, who are held out by their mentors to be the smart ones. The jealous types usually call them the whiz-kids, the fair-haired children and other, less positive nicknames. And you must recognize that they are probably smarter than the average bear and in some cases, just barely. But, they are not the true smarts ones.

Some people who rise rapidly through an organization, and thus suggest the outward appearance of possessing higher-than-normal intelligence, are simply connected. They have been selected, for any variety of reasons, to be groomed as the next generation of senior or executive management. Typically, they get very high marks on the personality side of their character, and may or may not have better-than-average intelligence. The simple fact that they are selected frequently paints them with a Teflon coating that prevents negatives from sticking, especially when it comes to their intelligence.

Most of these people who have been singled out for this rapid rise up the corporate ladder have the support of only one or two influential people. It might be because they are connected to someone else of importance— the owner's kid, the son or daughter of the president of the company's largest supplier or customer, someone with political connections. The fact is that these people usually are not selected because they really are the smart ones. We will talk more about these fast-trackers later. I introduced the concept here to draw a distinction between them and the real smart ones.

Personality quirks of the smart ones may include:

- Shyness

- The inability to work well with other team members

- Lack of political sensitivity

- Difficulty conforming to rules and guidelines

- Annoyance in having to slow down to let the rest of us catch up

- A seemingly endless supply of facts, figures, quotes, ideas, creative suggestions, and options, yet a limited amount of common sense or "street smarts"

The Smart One

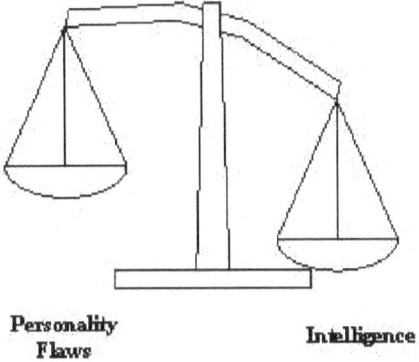

Personality
Flaws

Intelligence

I point these quirks out only to let you know that all too often, those who try to give the appearance of being especially smart—the fast-trackers—usually are not really the sharpest knives in the drawer. The truly smart ones are like most of us in that they possess a variety of skills and experiences, and balance them against their own personalities and characteristics. In their case, the intelligence side always comes up (or down if being measure on a the scale) as the strongest.

Almost every single highly intelligent person I've come across in the work environment eventually became someone I could deal with productively, and, in most cases, I can honestly say that we struck up a friendship. Now, that does not mean we went to the Star Trek conventions together dressed in our Klingon battle attire, but it does mean that we treated each other with respect, sought out each other's company at lunchtime, and made sure we were assigned to the same projects when and if possible.

To achieve maximum success in the workplace, you have to be willing to live with the personality quirks of others, and you must also recognize that, to others, you may also possess personality quirks of your own. Don't let those things that make us individuals get in the way of establishing relationships that will be beneficial to your success in business and to your own personal success as you seek growth opportunities.

Your Team Members

The Team Machine

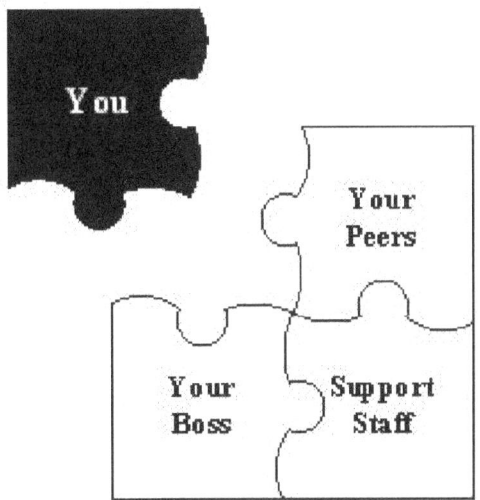

There are very few positions in which one is truly a sole contributor. Most positions are linked, however thinly, to the efforts of other positions. Your efforts are combined with those of others, with the end result being the goods or services offered by the enterprise. You rely on someone farther up the food chain, and those below you rely on you.

In a sales environment, the team begins with a lead salesperson. Others assist this person including:

- The boss

  o Assigns territories and accounts

  o Provides training and other skills-development tools

  o Oversees progress

  o Removes roadblocks

- Sales peers

  o Provide competitive motivation

  o Assist in sales strategy development

  o Suggest problem resolutions based upon their prior experiences

- Marketing staff

  o Provide background information on accounts

  o Assist in the development of sales presentations

- Production staff

  o Provide subject matter expertise to be used during sales calls

  o Produce mockups and samples

- Support staff

  o Develop pricing models

  o Write proposals

  o Ship requested samples

Even in a much less sophisticated environment where the key question asked by the salesperson is, "Do you want some fries with your hamburger?," someone else is usually behind the scenes salting the fries, flipping the burgers, ordering the buns, and cleaning the grease pit. So, it stands to reason that a team that functions together well will outperform a team that is dysfunctional.

That being said, we must also accept that we may not be in a position to choose whether or not we want to be on a particular team. And in most cases, we have no real decision-making power as to who the other team members are. Your role on the team is also an important consideration that needs to be explored, and your role may be one of the following:

- The team leader

- The team facilitator

- The subject matter expert

- The support person

- The workhorse

- The political eye candy

Based upon your role, you may be an active participant or someone who contributes only occasionally.

And even the nature of the team will vary in its mission and duration. Take the following teams, for example:

- A permanent team focused on improving plant efficiency

- A short-duration team focused on selling your firm's goods or services to the ABC account

- A permanent team working on short-term assignments like developing the new models for each year's sales campaigns

Through these examples, we can understand that teams do vary in purpose and that your assignment to a team may or may not be long-lasting. Further, many departments are structured so that the very nature of your position is to be a member of a permanent team. You may be the lead cost accountant in the firm's financial department: you are an integral cog in the effort to determine costs and profitability. The mission is clear and the duration of the position is permanent, even though your time in the position may not be.

As I said in the Introduction to this book, the vast majority of the people I encounter are typically decent, pleasant, and hard working. The same will probably hold true for you in terms of the people you will meet as you journey down the path you will look back upon one day and fondly remember as your career. You will become a member of a team, maybe many teams, throughout your career, and most of those experiences will be rewarding and pleasant.

An old saying points out that there is no *i* or *u* in *team*. Obviously this is literally true. Try using an *i* or *u* in the word and your spell checker will nail you every single time!

During the course of my career, I've heard a number of people use the phrase "my team." On the surface, so what? Unfortunately, some of the people who uttered that phrase truly believed that they, as the leaders, were the most important people on their teams. And while the leader may have the ultimate responsibility for the team's success or failure, at least from an accountability standpoint, I submit that the role of leader is no more important than that of any of the other roles that comprise the team. Is the leader's role more important than that of the workhorse, or the subject matter expert? Is providing the team with support and direction more important that actually solving the problem at hand? The point is that every position on a team is integral to the team's ability to generate a successful outcome. If a role isn't important to the outcome, is the role even necessary? On the other hand, remember the label "political eye candy" that we used earlier? This term describes the classic example of people who are on a team because their presence looks good, rather than because their contributions make a noticeable difference. Having the owner's dim-witted son on the team is an example of "political eye candy".

By and large, most people on a team are interested in contributing and are focused on being successful. Some of these people are drafted while others volunteer. In the end, only the final success or failure of the team is important to the organization. How well the team functions as a team in terms of its interpersonal dealings is usually only a matter of concern to the team members themselves. Most people, however, want a pleasant experience and work hard at making the team environment a painless undertaking.

The Mentor

About thirty months into my career, I moved from what is typically viewed as a staff position (an estimator) to a line position (sales representative). This was a real departure from my original plan, which was to work my way up through the administrative side of the business. But, nothing ventured, nothing gained, so I interviewed for the sales position and got it.

The company I worked for at the time had two types of sales representatives. In the first category were those whose income was commission driven (the more they sold, the more they made). These sales representatives were the ones who viewed themselves as the only true sales people. Hence, those making the most were the best of the best. In the second category, the one that I belonged to, were sales people who managed large, established house accounts. My compensation package included a salary plus a performance-based bonus. The consensus at the company was that those who couldn't really sell became part of the second category.

My first sales manager never should have been a manager in the first place. He had been a commissioned sales representative, the first one to work out of a home office for the company. Up until he opened his home office, all sales representatives worked out of company locations. He was a successful sales person, and his boss, the one who broke the mold and let a sales representative work out of a home office, eventually rewarded him by promoting him to sales management as a way of saying thanks.

Good sales people do not always make good sales managers, and my manager was a case in point—maybe even the poster child.

He just didn't have it. He could not train others, he could not see the bigger picture, and he wanted to do the sales person's job, not his job as manager. And it didn't take long for those of us who reported to him to do everything in our power to avoid him.

Fortunately for me, I happened to work in one of our largest sales offices. Between VPs, sales managers, sales representatives, and administrative assistants, there were around sixty people in the office. One of these individuals, Kent, was a sales manager in one of the other groups. His sales team was a commission-based sales force. To get to my office, I had to walk down a hallway that took me right past the door to his office. Because he was a manager he had a decent-sized office—with windows no less!

Kent, never known to be shy, jumped up from behind his desk the first time he laid eyes on me and, in a loud, boisterous voice said, "Aren't you house account humps supposed to be using the back door?" Anyone not seeing the smile on his face or the extended hand ready for a good, solid handshake might have taken the comment as an insult. Kent … well, Kent was just being Kent—big-hearted and fun-loving every single minute of the day. Even when he was angry and ranting, he seemed to have a mischievous glint in his wild Irish eyes.

After the initial handshake and introductions, we both continued on with our day. From that point on though, every time I walked past his office, I made it a point to look in. If he wasn't on the telephone or in a meeting, I'd stick my head in for a few minutes and chat. Over time, these chats became discussions, and, before I knew it, I began seeking his counsel on a problem—or he'd tell me about a new sales opportunity his team had uncovered in their market.

The Mentor

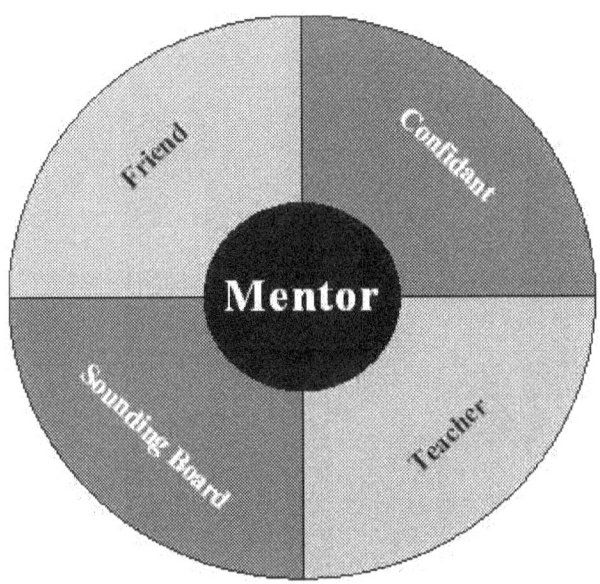

During one of the conversations Kent and I had, I made the mistake of complaining about my manager's lack of smarts and then froze, realizing that I was bad-mouthing one sales manager to another sales manager. Instead of giving me a reprimand, or even a raised eyebrow, Kent simply said, "I know what you mean. That's why I've been helping you." And Kent became my acknowledged mentor. A few weeks later, by the way, he did point out that my negative comments about my sales manager, though true, could get me into trouble if spoken to the wrong person. One of the benefits of having a mentor is getting great advice!

Having a mentor—someone truly interested in my development—was and continues to be a wonderful experience. First of all, having someone in your corner is always a plus. Second, recognizing that the mentor's interest in you is not self-serving but a genuine expression of his interest to help you adds a level of comfort that makes the mentor/mentored relationship pleasurable. Third, having someone in whom you can confide your innermost feelings is critical for your own peace of mind. And fourth, having someone who will give you an unbiased appraisal of ideas, concepts, and positions is invaluable to your development.

A good mentor will:

- Be there for you

- Explain his comments, suggestions, and recommendations

- Not have a hidden agenda regarding her reasons for helping you

- Not simply give you the answers, but help you reason them out for yourself

- Tell you when you're wrong

- Challenge you as he assists you

- Usually just becomes your mentor without coercion or without being asked

Now every Tom, Dick, and Harriet who offers to help you isn't necessarily a mentor. And even some of the people who volunteer to help you with a call-me-at-any-time-if-I-can-help comment really don't want to be mentors. Many simply want to wrap themselves in a cloak of political correctness, hoping that you never do ask them for help. And sometimes, when you do ask them for help, you find that they really can't help or, worse, are unwilling to help. So, when you can chose a mentor, chose wisely.

And who can be a mentor? A mentor can be …

- Young, middle-aged, or old

- Male or female

- From any ethnic background

- College educated or a graduate of the school of hard knocks

- Above, equal to, or below you in position

- An extrovert or an introvert

In other words, a mentor can be almost anyone—but not just anyone can be a mentor.

A mentor really wants to help the person he is mentoring. A positive mentoring relationship can grow from any number of circumstances. Sometimes one person may be assigned to mentor another. Or two people who just happen to like each other may develop a spontaneous mentor relationship. However it happens, the mentoring relationship can become one of the strongest that develops in the business environment, and it may be equally rewarding for both the mentor and the person being mentored.

Kent and I became fast friends. And because we both worked for the same company at the same location, we saw each other frequently. As time marched on, Kent left our company to join another firm, and eventually he moved on to establish his own business as an executive recruiter. After I left the company where we'd met, I called on Kent in his recruiting business and told him my tale of woe. Within two weeks, he found me a great position at a company that was a competitor to our former employer. Several years after that, I used his services to find a couple of people I needed to hire. Thus we expanded our mentor relationship to a mutually beneficial business relationship.

Later, as I contemplated starting my own consulting business, Kent once again slipped into the role of mentor and helped me talk through the idea, review my business plan, and generally get the whole effort going. While others helped in one area or another, Kent was there every step of the way.

Kent is my mentor, my friend, a member of my network, and the big brother I never had.

The Boss

Like mentors, bosses come in all shapes, sizes, and dispositions, and bring different experience levels to the table.

A good boss has many attributes and, fortunately, I have had some terrific bosses over the years. I've also had some real jerks, but we will cover those characters in other parts of this book.

Good bosses usually rely on their own personal growth experiences in developing their "boss personas," but are also secure enough to know that they, too, can benefit from continued exposure to new ideas, procedures, and techniques. The good bosses will continually seek out additional developmental opportunities to help you, your team members, and themselves continue to grow, individually as well as collectively. And, above all else, they will make sure that you and your teammates have everything necessary to ensure your collective success. This includes education, training, equipment, access to data, access to other resources, the proper working environment, and anything else appropriate.

Boss as Leader

The position your boss fills should be respected. This does not mean that the person filling the position automatically deserves to be respected. It would be nice if only good people became bosses, but that isn't always the case.

Even if you respect your boss, you may not always agree with everything she says, but your respect for her position will enable you to work with her as the lead member of your team. You follow your boss's lead. We call these people leaders. One of the better bosses I had continually told us that he didn't want to be a good boss—he simply wanted to be a good leader. I truly believe there is a distinction, one that bad bosses either cannot seem to grasp, or chose to ignore.

A boss who is a leader will:

- Make sure you and your colleagues understand the goals and objectives that your team is responsible for, and include you in the development of strategies and tactics that you will need in order to accomplish your mission

- Provide you and your colleagues with the tools necessary to succeed, including such things as proper training, systems, and financial support.

- Act as the champion remover of roadblocks

- Constructively critique direction and performance

- Keep you focused

- Keep you motivated

- Earn your respect

Boss as Coach

One of the most important responsibilities of any boss is to train the people who work under him. Sometimes the boss does the training, either one-on-one, or in a group situation. Other times someone other than the boss does the training. But, at the end of the day, the boss is responsible for making sure that his direct reports are properly trained.

Once the employee learns the technical aspects of an assignment, whether it's learning how to interact with customers or how to use the accounting department's computer programs, the role of the good boss migrates from teacher to coach. The boss steps back a little, as the sun partly hidden behind the cloud in our graphic suggests, and watches the employee perform his responsibilities. From time to time the boss interjects comments, provides guidance in response to questions, and helps to identify solutions to seemingly insurmountable challenges. Like the coach of a sports team, the boss doesn't play the game—he coaches. He stands witness to what is happening around him, sending in the plays from time to time, and making sure all players are fulfilling their roles.

The two greatest responsibilities of the coach are to motivate and to act as the eyes and ears of the team.

The concept of motivation is straightforward in terms of understanding the meaning of the word. There are many ways to motivate, and we won't go through them here.

Suffice it to say that motivated people perform better than unmotivated people. A good boss recognizes this and does everything in his power to motivate his team and ensure the greatest chance for success in completing the mission at hand. The good boss motivates his team to perform at the peak of their ability.

Being the eyes and ears of the team is a different way of saying that the good boss also has a "big picture" view of what's happening on the field. Individual team members may be focused on individual tasks. The boss, however, is able to stand on the sidelines, take in all of the action and, through the application of gentle pressure, control the ebb and flow of the game.

Coaches congratulate players on a job well done and help console players when victory eludes their grasp.

Coaches help players find that extra effort required when energy is exhausted.

And coaches help members understand why their individual contributions are critical to the overall success of the team.

Boss as Boss

There are times when a boss simply needs to be a boss—a traffic cop or a referee.

Every company, organization, department, and team has rules. Some rules are written, while others are more informal. In either case, if a team member steps outside the line, it's the boss's job to let him know he's gone astray. He should expect to be called on the carpet—or worse, if he's committed a big enough offense.

A good boss knows when to don the referee's stripped shirt or pick up the cop's baton. He knows when to assign a simple time-out and when to hit an employee over the head!

The biggest difference between the good boss and bad boss is that the good boss rarely needs to fulfill the role of simply being the boss. The good boss is a leader and a coach. The good boss has earned the respect of those he manages. The bad boss, on the other hand, is almost always cast in the role of a simply being the boss or rule enforcer. Since he cannot coach and is not a leader, he has very little to offer. He simply enforces the rules.

The Customer

When I first accepted a position in line sales, my new sales manager accompanied me on my first introductory trip to the largest of my assigned house accounts. My company had been doing business with this particular customer for over thirty years and I was the next in a long line of junior sales people to be introduced to the account. The first person we met was the department head of the group of people that actually were our customers—the buyers of the services we provided. My manager introduced me to this gentleman, who was approximately fifty years old at the time.

"You don't look Irish," was his opening comment to me. (Many people assume that because of the way my last name, Bragen, sounds, I must be of Irish extraction.)

"Actually, even though you can't tell by the spelling of my name, my family's Polish," was my response.

The customer's face immediately changed from a tight-lipped grimace to a wide-open, tooth-filled smile. "Me, too, kid. Me, too. I think we're going to get along just fine. Call me Ziggy."

Now, the first thing about that short story is that it's the god's honest truth. Ziggy really was Polish, with a last name that started with the letter *Z*, followed by several *Cs*, *Ys*, a *G* and a *T*. Not only was the name virtually unpronounceable, I never heard anyone actually use it when addressing him. In fact, Ziggy had a corkboard up on his office wall and attached to it with pushpins and thumbtacks were numerous envelopes, faxes, and address labels, all addressed to him. Not a single one displaying the proper spelling of his name!

The reality about a line sales position, where you are actually in face-to-face contact with customers and prospects, is that no matter how much training you may have had, no matter how many books you've read—including my first book, *A Beginner's Guide to a Successful Career*, which has a whole section devoted to sales skills—the only real way to learn selling is to start doing it.

That meeting with Ziggy was my first sales call ever and, because we made a simple connection over our shared ethnic heritage, it went well for me. Over the next few months, Ziggy took me under his wing so he could "teach me the ropes." We became pretty good friends and a part of each other's networks. He introduced me to the right people, told me what it took to close the deal, helped me advance in my career, and kept me out of trouble—except when we shared the three-martini lunches that were so popular thirty years ago.

Ziggy did all of this for two reasons. First, I really think he liked me. I sure know I liked him. These mutual feelings lasted until he died of cancer. The second reason Ziggy helped me was symbiotic in nature. By nurturing me, he was creating a staunch supporter: me. There wasn't anything I wouldn't do for Ziggy short of breaking the law. I was there for him and his company each and every time. In retrospect, he sold me on himself—a very astute business move on his part.

The focused commitment to aid and assist the customer is what separates the truly extraordinary sales person from the average sales person. And while I would not argue against that point, my relationship with Ziggy transcended even that level of sales person/customer relationship. I still remember him fondly and thank him for all of the help he was able and willing to offer me throughout those formative years of my selling career.

To avoid painting a picture that isn't completely accurate, let me also share the downside of such a close relationship.

Ziggy was still the customer, and the customer is always right, even when he's dead wrong. And, Ziggy possessed a temper. When he kept his ego in check, he was a very pleasant fellow to be around. But when things didn't go his way and his ego emerged, I had to mind my *Ps* and *Qs* because he would jump up on the stage, hold court, and expect everyone to bow before the king.

The strength and depth of our relationship also resulted in his expectation that I always be available for him, whether it was to sit at the bar all night with him while he regaled me with stories about years gone by, or to respond to his pounding on my hotel room door at three in the morning because he was too drunk to remember where he parked the car and wanted me to drive him home.

So, Ziggy, the Polish fellow with the unpronounceable name, was human like the rest. But I still acknowledge that, compared to any other customer I ever dealt with in the years that followed, he taught me more about selling and more about dealing with unique characters than anyone else, and for that I will always have a warm spot in my heart for poor old Ziggy.

During the course of my selling career, first as a sales representative, then as a sales manager, then VP, Sr. VP, and eventually group president, I must have encountered hundreds of customers, and through their organizations, probably met another thousand or so people. Most seemed pleasant, though they left no lasting impression. Some did leave an impression—a mixture of The Good, The Bad and The Ugly. Since this section of the book addresses The Good, I will continue on with a few more of the positive examples. We will cover the others in their appropriate sections.

The second account that I was introduced to was another major customer of the firm and, once again, we'd been doing business with this company for a long time. My first meeting took place in St. Louis, which at the time was their headquarter location. Our company was about to start the annual production of their largest orders, and they were going to send us several women who would be involved in a quality check process during the production run. As the new sales representative on the account, it was my job to meet these women at the airport, get them situated in a hotel, get them to the plant, act as customer/plant liaison, take them to dinner, and serve as around-the-clock gofer.

So there I was, twenty-seven years old, relatively fresh out of university, very fresh in a new sales position—and faced with the responsibility of interacting with three representatives of a large customer for an extended period of time. My first thoughts upon receiving the assignment were, "What the heck am I going to talk to these women about over dinner. I don't know anything about cooking, or sewing, or the women's liberation movement. I don't know nuthin' 'bout birthin' no babies!" (Some readers may remember that last part from *Gone With the Wind.*)

Now before anyone jumps down my throat, I know … that was a very chauvinistic attitude and I will be the first one to admit that, at the time, I was extremely naive in my way of thinking. In my defense, I will share that my entire sales training class had been comprised of men, my department was populated with men, except for the female secretaries, and that virtually all of my other customer contacts were male.

To put the icing on the cake, I had just been married. This work assignment called for me to attend four dinners on consecutive nights, the last one on the Fourth of July, a day that found the plant, the three women, and me all working a full day. Let us just say that this week promised to be difficult at best, and at worse, the potential end of either my sales career or my marriage!

Though I was dreading it, the first day's activities rushed by and I found myself in the car with the three female customers on our way to dinner. I was so new in sales that it hadn't even dawned on me to ask them what they might like for dinner. I simply picked my favorite restaurant, which happened to be a place that specialized in seafood. It was only after the menus were passed out that one of the women, in a heavy Texas accent, said that she never, ever in her life had eaten any kind of seafood and was not about to start tonight. Before I could even start to mutter an apology, one of the other women piped up, "Now, Jessie, don't be ridiculous. There's nothing wrong with seafood." And with that icebreaker, we started an evening-long conversation about food, our upbringings, our fondest childhood memories, our work experiences, our marriages, their children, and so on. It was a truly delightful evening. The dinner on the Fourth of July was even better. We went to a restaurant in the Hancock Building in Chicago and ate dinner at a restaurant on the ninety-sixth floor. At around nine-thirty we watched the City of Chicago's lakefront fireworks display. We were so high up in the building that many of the fireworks and skyrockets were actually exploding below our level. It was truly amazing.

These women, too, taught me an extremely valuable lesson. At every dinner we attended, they asked me why I hadn't brought my wife. My response was the response that my manager had drilled into my head: "She had something already on the calendar and couldn't make it." Well, she didn't really have anything going on, but my manager trained me not to include my spouse. It was the same with all of the other sales representatives under him: no spouses. He didn't feel it was appropriate to include spouses on the company check, and also felt that their presence acted as a deterrent to conducting business. At the time, it made sense to me. It was only after years of arguments with my wife that I truly understood how stupid that rule was, and how much I truly had wanted to involve my wife. Unfortunately, by that time, she really did have other commitments on the calendar and she ended up participating in far too few entertainment situations where her presence would have been a big plus.

The last of my accounts that we will discuss involved a situation in which a contact of mine in Ohio accepted a promotion to a role at the Michigan headquarters of a new company formed through the combination of his previous employer with four other Great Lakes companies. I happened to be the sales representative assigned to this new, expanded account, so we were able to continue our relationship.

Over the course of time, we became good friends—this time with wives included. Al and I worked on what was the largest deal of its kind in the industry: a ten-year contract worth in excess of one billion dollars. And that was way back in the '80s, when a billion-dollar customer/supplier contract was big stuff, especially in our industry.

To this day, the four of us remain good friends. We've stuck together through thick and thin. Al and his wife Kathy agreed to be our daughter's godparents. Al helped me through a career crisis, and I helped Al find employment when his company underwent a restructuring, leaving him out in the cold.

THE BAD

People you will want to avoid if possible

The Loudmouth

There are two typical definitions of the term "loudmouth" and we will explore both, as both versions can be mildly irritating in some cases and aggravating and embarrassing in extreme cases.

The first loudmouth we will look at displays the literal meaning of this word, and is simply a person who speaks with a very loud voice. I don't mean the person who shouts out with an occasional outburst or someone who just happens to laugh too loudly. I mean the kind of person who is always loud. In spite of the already high noise level, you can tell that Sally or Steve is in the room because of their voice, which you can clearly hear above everyone else's.

When I first started working, I was assigned to a small team that had a loudmouth as one of its members. He was a pretty decent guy—married, a couple kids, a mortgage, and dreams like the rest of us. Unfortunately, his whisper was a roar and his normal speaking voice was even louder. He was continually asked by many people, even those across the crowded bullpen office space that housed twenty-five of us, to keep his voice down. Even his performance review contained comments about his volume.

His loudness irritated people. It made people shy away from him because, no matter what he was talking about, or who he was talking with, everybody in the area got the gist of the conversation because when good old Steve started talking, he sounded like the barker in a sideshow. We never quite figured out why he did this. We do believe it was unconscious on his part. And, as I said earlier, he was a pretty decent fellow, but most of us maintained only an arm's length relationship with the guy. He wasn't part of any networks, frequently ate lunch alone, and wasn't invited to many after-hours gatherings—all because of his volume level. Since being friends with Steve was a struggle, he didn't have many friends, at least at work.

While this poor unfortunate, and those like him, make for uncomfortable relationships, the second kind of loudmouth is even more frustrating, and is potentially damaging to your career.

The second kind of loudmouth we'll look at actually speaks with a normal volume and doesn't scream or yell or even talk loudly. This loudmouth is an information megaphone, broadcasting the contents of every conversation to everyone else, and, even more unfortunate and damaging, citing the sources of all that's broadcast.

In other words, these people don't acknowledge and/or respect any level of confidence you have placed in them, and, in fact, inherently think that just because you said something to them, it is understood and agreeable to you that they are free to repeat the remarks to others and attribute the comments to you.

Clearly, there are times when we all do this: "I asked Barney where he wanted to go to lunch and he suggested the pizza parlor. That okay with you?"

There are times though when it's not acceptable and can be very damaging: "I think that dress looks great on you but Barney thinks it makes your butt look even bigger."

Beyond these somewhat humorous examples are some potentially very damaging possibilities as well. You frequently share comments about this person or that person with your co-workers. You share opinions about bosses, about other co-workers, about religion and politics and financial matters.

As we continue to develop relationships with people, we naturally extend our trust boundaries and share more and more, until one day we share the wrong thing with the wrong person and it comes back to haunt us.

And while this is bad, the scenarios presented thus far are the good ones in the sense that, when you eventually learn which people are information megaphones, you start to become very circumspect with the information you share with them.

The Machiavellians among us may even see this as an opportunity to plant false information in an attempt to use these information megaphones as a positive force in our own individual quest to move onward and upward.

But the worst scenario is the damage that occurs when you don't know you're communicating with an information megaphone. In a later section we will discuss the most obvious of these—the spy who is working towards his or her own hidden agenda.

What motivates people to operate in this manner? We will explore several possible reasons:

Political Motivation

Most people want to get ahead at what they're doing, whether it's on the job or in their personal pursuits. This is why we study, practice, and try hard to do things well. We want the personal satisfaction of having done a good job, and we want the accolades that accrue, be they salary increases, promotions, or just the simple admiration and/or acknowledgement that we receive from people whose comments we value.

So, to some degree, we are all politically motivated in the work environment, even though all of us may not want the job as president, or even want the headaches and heartaches that come with being promoted up one level from our current position. We want to be acknowledged for our contributions, we want to be satisfied with our own sense of accomplishing what constitutes our personal work ethic, and we want to be viewed by our peers as a valued member of the team.

There are those, however, whose sense of political motivation far exceeds their true concern for others, and they are willing to do whatever they have to do to get ahead. Some of these people don't have the skills to hide their true motivation and they wear their hidden agendas on their sleeves. These people are obvious with their I'm-the-only-one-who-counts mannerisms. While you need to be aware of these people, it's fairly easy to identify them and either stay clear or at least be guarded in your personal interactions with them. On the other hand, there are those politically motivated types who are able to wrap themselves in a shroud of the common man. These people work behind the scenes to improve their own image, often at the expense of others.

Whether people are open or secretive about their political motivation, they will use what you tell them, either openly or in confidence, as a simple bartering chip as they vie for positions of favor among the more influential members of the organization. If they can make points by revealing what they heard from someone else, they will. And even if they can't increase their own points, they will use what you shared with them to your detriment in an effort to make you lose points. Also, many a great idea, uttered by someone in seeming confidence, becomes the usurped property of the loudmouth, who does not hesitate, especially if politically motivated, to represent the idea as his own.

Information is Power

Just about everyone has heard this phrase before and some will refine it even further by saying that *applied* information is power.

In either case, information is power, and many people truly believe they become more powerful by having more information at their fingertips. They absorb information like sponges and squirrel it away for future use. Some of them actually take the time necessary to make sure they understand the information, for in understanding comes true power. But not all information sponges worry about that.

Information sponges seek out and absorb all of the information they can. In fact, their mission becomes much more important than the information itself, or their personal understanding of that information. This is why many information sponges take things out of context. They listen to a five-minute conversation and walk away with what they feel is a pearl of wisdom, the important fact, or the self-confessed sin. Then, in a different conversation, they reach back and pick up your statement about not liking the new boss, or not agreeing with the department's strategy, or not liking all of the overtime required by the new project, and they lob it like a hand grenade into a completely different conversation.

This type of loudmouth—the information-is-power town crier—becomes your worst enemy, misstating your words, coloring your intentions, taking comments out of context, and representing your humor as fact-based attacks against someone. This loudmouth will besmirch your reputation, not because she doesn't like you and is trying to tear you down, but just because she doesn't clearly understand the power that information can have, especially information that is taken out of context, or is misspoken. And before you know it, someone up the food chain all of a sudden does not like you, or you're not given the new project, raise or promotion, and you cannot figure out why.

Social Unconsciousness

Though we will discuss stupid people in more detail later, we must say here that some people are just stupid when it comes to protecting the identity of who originated a statement or comment. These people feel that just because they heard person A say something, they have some inherent right or permission to attribute that statement to person A when speaking with person B. They don't recognize the need for information flow control, and anything that gets said to them becomes immediately available for regurgitation to others.

You lean over to Mike and whisper that the boss's suit looks a little tight around the middle and the next thing you know, Mike is talking loud enough to be heard by many, saying that Tim thinks the boss is getting fat and his clothes don't fit anymore!

Everyone nods off once in a while when it comes to social consciousness. We all make mistakes, wishing we could take back something that we said in haste, anger, jest, or simple social unconsciousness. Some people just seem as if they never wake up, almost seeming to prefer to stumble through life, saying whatever whenever, not understanding the consequences of their words.

As to how to deal with a loudmouth you might want to consider the following:

- Once you have identified the loudmouth(s) in your organization, be circumspect in the information you choose to share with them.

- If you do want the world to know something, the quickest way to communicate it is through a loudmouth.

- Listen carefully, but with a grain of salt, to what the loudmouth is broadcasting as you may gain some valuable insights and tidbits of information.

- If you are in a supervisory role, think twice about moving a loudmouth into a line sales role as their future actions may end up costing you a customer or two.

The Know-It-All

The character of Cliff the mailman on the television series *Cheers* is a classic, though humorous, example of a know-it-all. Whatever Cliff doesn't know, he simply makes up—sometimes even making up the words that support his explanation of things!

Most of us enjoy a good laugh, and having a Cliff character around for entertainment, especially at the lunch table or on a business trip, can help the time fly by. But having to work with a know-it-all who isn't simply trying to be funny can be difficult at best and a real career killer at worst.

There is a big difference between a know-it-all and someone who is truly intelligent and in command of the facts. Both give the impression that they know the answers, but only one really does. And the one who really does know a lot of answers will simply say, "I don't know," when she doesn't—she won't make up some nonsensical answer.

Using a know-it-all as a source of information or confirmation of information is like asking a blind man to pick out the red ball amongst several hundred white balls, or asking a deaf man to tell you who is singing that song, or expecting a politically insensitive author to use a politically sensitive example. Most of the time, you will be deeply disappointed with the result of using a know-it-all as a source of useable information. If it isn't a big deal, who cares? But if it is a (literal) big deal, you could lose it … and it could cost you your job.

Know-it-alls are usually well known by the group. You will hear people making comments to you in an effort to warn you about Bob or Ida. You will see people avoiding them when possible and limiting their contact to only the most superficial issues when contact is required. Keep your eyes and ears open, and you will soon know whom to avoid.

The new person coming into the organization could also be a know-it-all, one who has yet to be identified so pay attention.

Everyone has opinions on at least some issues. There are times when we may not have enough information about something to have an opinion, or at least not an informed opinion, but that may not stop us from voicing an opinion. And since many of us stake out positions and opinions with a certain amount of passion, it may be difficult to distinguish a highly opinionated person from a know-it-all. But I say someone who seems to be highly opinionated about everything is probably a know-it-all in training, and he himself may not even recognize the fact, which is interestingly ironic.

A know-it-all can bring disastrous harm to an organization. Here are but a few choice examples:

- The know-it-all sales manager accompanies a neophyte sales person on a visit to a new prospect. The sales person asks some interesting probing questions to elicit information from the prospective client. Instead of keeping his mouth shut and letting the prospective client answer the questions, the know-it-all sales manager answers the questions for the prospect. The sales person walks away from the meeting thinking she knows the prospect's thoughts on these matters. But in reality, all she knows is what her manager said. The result: the sales person develops an account sales strategy that may not be successful.

- In a blue-sky idea development meeting, the know-it-all presents an idea that he defends passionately, eventually persuading the group to adopt it as the group position. Only later does the group learn that the know-it-all's real understanding of the proposed solution is flawed and the project falls behind schedule, costing the company a lot of money.

- The know-it-all customer contact tells you "all you need to know" to make a big sale to her company. She shares pricing information, performance standards, and credit terms. You develop a proposal based upon this information, only to find most of it was inaccurate. Unfortunately, you don't learn about the inaccuracies until after your competitor is awarded the business.

So you try to avoid the know-it-alls, and make sure you're cautious in dealing with them when you cannot. But how do you deal with them when you have to?

The following safeguards will go a long way in minimizing your risks when the situation forces you to deal with a know-it-all:

- Document all information you receive from a know-it-all, even the simple stuff, so you have a paper trail that documents what was said by whom.

- Seek confirmation from other (reliable) informed sources on all points made by the know-it-all.

- Make sure your immediate supervisor is aware that the person you're dealing with is a know-it-all, but be careful. It's best, of course, if your supervisor already recognizes the know-it-all's tactics. If she doesn't, make sure you expose her to the know-it-all in a situation where she can witness her in action first-hand, eliminating the necessity for you to be a "tattle-tale." As a last resort, you may have to tell your supervisor outright that you're dealing with a know-it-all and ask for assistance in helping to separate fact from fiction.

The Drunk

First and foremost, this section isn't a diatribe against the evils of alcohol. Everyone should decide what is and what isn't acceptable behavior, within the limits of the law, when it comes to drinking—especially when driving is involved. Alcoholism has been called a disease. I won't debate that and I'm sure that there are both physical and mental dynamics that form the basis for this label. But in the grand scheme of things, you will come across a broad based group of drinkers during your career including alcoholics, heavy drinkers, social drinkers, and once-in-a-blue-moon drinkers. I pass no judgment on any of these drinkers, good or bad. We're simply going to explore them in the context of understanding them as you interact with them on the job.

Second, because a person is an alcoholic or heavy drinker does not mean you'll always encounter him stumbling around, spouting slurred speech.

And, remember an important fact about alcoholics: there are those who drink and those who no longer drink. Some have managed to live with the condition by abstaining, while others cannot wait until the next swig. Yet, both can and do function in the workplace, and some are able to do so without negatively impacting the operation, or the lives of their co-workers.

In the case of non-drinking alcoholics, it should be pretty obvious that they have made the conscious decision to stop consuming alcohol and, as a result, while they may still wear the alcoholic label, they are really non-drinkers. We should admire the willingness of these people to adhere to their abstinence commitment, and we should do what we can to support them, if we know about their condition. In many cases, we don't know. People abstain from consuming alcohol for a variety of reasons including religion, diet, personal preference, and alcoholism. Whatever the reason, we should simply acknowledge that it is an individual choice as to whether or not people consume alcohol.

I'm not sure what the boundary is between still-drinking alcoholics and heavy drinkers, but these individuals, though they attempt to mask their issues, can have a negative impact on the business that employs them, and on you as a co-worker as well. These people do tend to let their obsession with alcohol cloud their judgment, and the result is often a decrease in their performance level on the job. If they hold a desk job, it could mean the loss of a big deal, a setback that could be traced back to a damaging inappropriate comment, or a missed deadline that has a snowball effect. If they hold a job that involves heavy machinery, or transporting people, or providing screenings at the airport, a lack of focus or poor job performance can result in injury and even death—a very sobering thought, yet not sobering enough to encourage some drinkers to not place the lives of others in jeopardy.

When you see old Joe or Tina roll into work in the morning with blood-shot eyes, a tired looking face, or any other visible symptoms that suggest a brain-shattering headache, and the definite smell of alcohol oozing out of their pours, you might shake you head in disgust, or snicker to yourself. Your working environment may make the drunk's presence in that condition a moot point. The drunk may be a solitary contributor, whose efforts—pro or con—have no impact on you as an individual or on you as part of a larger team. But somewhere in the grand scheme of things, the drunk is wasting the corporation's money.

There are other times where the impact of the drunk on the business is immediate and far reaching. In any situation when the productivity of each and every team member is paramount, the poor performance of one reflects on the productivity of the whole. Numerous examples can be used to demonstrate this and I will suggest only a few of the more obvious: the impact potential is obviously huge if it's the pilot, surgeon, lead defense counsel, or O-ring inspector who is distracted because of a crippling hangover, or whose reactions are slowed because of the effect of residual alcohol in the body.

Some organizations and bosses put up with this type of behavior from the heavy drinkers for several reasons:

- There is a misguided feeling that employees are family and the company takes care of its own, paying the drinker instead of casting her out of the family.

- The boss likes the individual, and has a history with him.

- The organization refuses to acknowledge the problem.

- The organization does not know how to handle the problem.

So, now that we can see that this issue exists, and can see the severe impacts it can have on individuals as well as organizations, what should we do?

This is a question with many answers. In some industries, I imagine there are some rather specific, highly enforceable rules. If you see a pilot drinking a few beers on his way to the airplane, tell someone. (If you work for the airline and see this behavior, it may even be a requirement to tell someone.) If you see a heavy machine operator have a few shots at lunch and then return to work to operate a stamping machine that shapes flat sheet metal, tell someone.

On the other hand, if you see a fellow office worker drinking a beer with lunch, or see the boss's executive assistant having a glass of wine at lunch, don't go running back saying Peter or Anna is a drunk.

Use some common sense in this area. Ultimately, the only person you can truly control is yourself.

And while this section deals exclusively with alcohol, substance abuse of any kind also mirrors the personality types we have covered, and should be addressed in a similar fashion.

The Empty Suit

At the other end of the spectrum from Mr. Know-It-All, meet Mr. I-Don't-Know, also known as the empty suit.

Every organization has at least one empty suit—and sometimes, quite a few. Though our graphic here is a representation of a man's suit, this phenomenon does not recognize any boundaries based upon gender, hence you'll find some female empty suits out there, too.

Rarely is someone an empty suit from the get-go. Empty suits have usually been hired because of their skills. After some training and on-the-job experience, they typically become contributing members of the enterprise. At some point during their careers, for several reasons that we will explore later in this section, these people, who have been productive, all of a sudden seem to forget everything they have learned. As if someone locked a door and threw away the key, these people cannot seem to remember anything, make a decision, or render an informed opinion. They simply exist from day to day, going through the motions without making a real contribution. And the almost unbelievable aspect of these situations is that, in many cases, the organization tolerates this behavior, usually not even recognizing it.

Situations that can trigger the creation of an empty suit include:

- Promotion to or above the individual's Peter Principle level, where one achieves a position higher than their true capabilities

- Transfer of a person into one area based upon seniority or past job performance in a completely different area (for example, a sales manager becomes the accounting department manager)

- Any event that leads to a personal breakdown, which may not have any outward signs other than the empty suit syndrome

- A person's conscious decision to rest on past laurels and milk the system

A classic example that I witnessed time after time is the promotion of a great sales person into the role of sales manager. The skills and experiences that make a great sales person are not necessarily the same skills and experiences that make a great sales manager.

Sales people typically sell. They uncover opportunities, develop relationships, make sales presentations, and close deals. Sales manager do many other things in addition to helping make sales. The following list is taken from my first book, *A Beginner's Guide to a Successful Career* and, though far from complete, is indicative of the differences in the roles of sales representative and sales manager. A manager's responsibilities include:

- Developing personal relationships with key customers

- Interviewing and hiring new sales people

- Authoring or assisting in the development of job descriptions for sales and sales-related staff positions

- Developing or helping to develop compensation plans

- Training and developing skills of sales people and those in related staff positions

- Developing and implementing both strategic and tactical plans for expanding the sales unit's customer base

- Creating, or assisting in the development of, collateral support material, advertising messages, and/or marketing messages

- Interacting with other company-wide departments on behalf of the sales unit to solve problems and overcome hurdles

- Developing, or assisting in the development of, trade show and convention themes, display booths, and customer and prospect entertainment venues

- Forecasting future sales opportunities to coincide with annual budget development efforts

- Establishing and monitoring annual sales unit expense budgets

- Documenting performance and providing performance improvement information to direct reports

- Overseeing the proper calculation and processing of commission and/or bonus payments to sales people

- Assisting in developing an awareness of market trends, to be used by the company to develop future goods and services in anticipation of changing market needs

- Motivating the sales unit to higher levels of performance

- Participating in management of the sales unit office needs including:

  o Floor space

  o Furniture

  o Equipment and office supplies

  o Computers—both hardware and software

  o Staffing

  o Heating, air conditioning, electricity, etc.

- Oh, yeah, and helping to make some sales!

Early in my sales career, one of my first sales managers would have been a perfect poster boy for the role of empty suit. He was a nice enough guy, had fairly decent relationships with our customers, and could help us sales representatives out on account-related problems. But when it came to market assessments, new product strategies, budgeting, marketing, advertising, hiring, and training … well, he fell short. So short that, after a while, his reps deserted him in search of another sales manager who could provide some behind-the-scenes help in our development. You might consider rereading the Mentor chapter in The Good section. Kent was the person I sought out.

The little cartoon at the beginning of this section is obviously an empty suit; real empty suits are not always so easy to spot. Some of them have developed a camouflage that makes them appear to be contributing members of the organization. Here are some examples of typical empty suits:

Example #1—The Empty Suit Donning the Suit of the Mentor

While we all ask these types of questions or statements some of the time, an empty suit who is trying to hide by using the garb of the mentor always responds to a question you have asked with one of the following questions or statements:

- What do you think we should do?

- What are the options you've identified?

- Have you asked Raul, or Carol (or some other person in the organization) and, if you have, what answer did you get?

- Let's go see what Jim has to say about this.

- Have you scheduled a meeting with so-and-so to gather more input?

Invariably, the empty suit masquerading as a mentor will grab on to one or more of your own answers to answer your initial query and then will suggest that as a solution, which accomplishes several additional issues at the same time:

- The empty suit has given the appearance of providing you with guidance.

- If the answer the empty suit gives you works, she appears to be smart.

- If the answer the empty suit gives you fails, his fall back is that he was using the situation as a training device, or that you had not given him all of the pertinent facts necessary to provide a "correct" answer in the first place, or the delivery of the "correct" answer was handled "incorrectly."

In other words, no matter what the outcome, the empty suit is able to maintain an image of active participation and contribution, while really not adding anything of use to the overall effort.

Example #2—The Empty Suit Donning the Suit of the Clown

Humor clearly has its place in both our business and personal lives. Without humor, we would not have very much fun, now would we? Yet, humor is one of the easiest disguises for an empty suit to hide behind.

Even an empty suit knows some things, and feels very comfortable contributing what she knows. After all, it is a great way for an empty suit to appear normal if she can actually contribute something once in a while. And when she doesn't know something, or doesn't have anything meaningful to offer, many empty suits turn to humor as a distraction. While everyone is laughing, the spotlight usually turns to someone else in the conversation because someone will say something—anything—in response to the humorous comment. This person's comments will relieve the empty suit of the burden of having to give a serious and meaningful response to a question she cannot answer.

Not everyone who uses humor is an empty suit. This is an obvious statement. Yet, an empty suit that uses humor as camouflage isn't always easy to identify. If someone uses humor in all serious situations, there may be a more serious issue that he is struggling to keep hidden.

Sooner or later, most people start to recognize that the empty suit is truly empty. Many times, empty suits are exposed, eventually labeled as performance problems, and either demoted or let go. Other times, they survive. Here are several reasons why they survive:

- If the boss is the empty suit, he will be insulated by the good performance of those he manages. Those above the empty suit figure that Leo must be good. Look at his numbers. Leo is also doing a good job in claiming credit for the successes and assigning blame for the failures. He continues to project the image of being the great leader, even though he really isn't pulling his weight.

- If the empty suit was previously a great contributor, the boss may turn a blind eye to her shortcomings and continue to tolerate her poor performance because of past accomplishments.

- If the empty suit has become a pro at deflecting suspicion, he can operate for years without fear of detection. These people tend to become invisible to the organization. You see them, they appear busy, and they talk up a good game. Yet no one seems to know what they really contribute, and when you need them for a project, or an answer, or anything of substance, they cannot be found. They really have developed their survival instinct and seem to just disappear within the organization. And the bigger the organization, the easier it is to hide. These individuals are often referred to as being in the coasting mode—toward retirement, often referred to as being retired in place.

In order to avoid any problems when encountering an empty suit, consider the following strategies:

- Don't ask the empty suit for help, expecting a meaningful contribution … it won't happen.

- Since empty suits tend to speak in generalisms, everything they say has the general appearance of being useful, but don't be lulled into a false sense of security and accept their answers with regard to questions of specificity.

- Most empty suits were at one time contributing members of the organization. If you uncover the subject in which he is truly an expert, he could be used as a source of information. To be on the safe side, double check the information they offer you with another subject matter expert before applying it as a solution to a problem.

The Fanatic

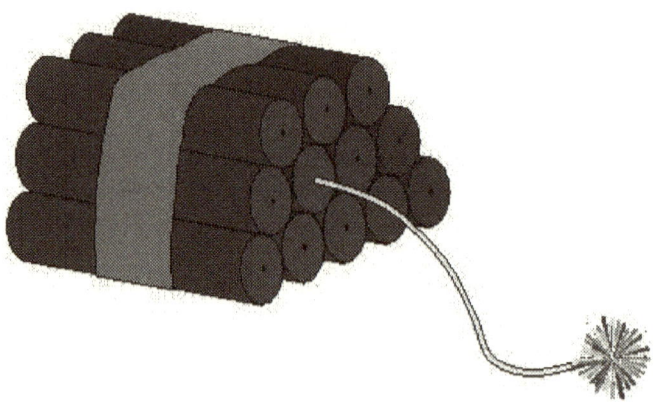

Everyone has personal beliefs and opinions, except maybe that 1.5 percent of the population who respond to opinion poll questions with answers such as "I don't know," or "I have no opinion." We also have varying degrees of conviction regarding those opinions. I might prefer chocolate ice cream to vanilla ice cream but, in the end, ice cream is ice cream and any flavor will do, thank you very much. On other subjects my level of conviction can be higher or lower, and there are some topics, such as protecting my children against anything that might bring them harm, that raise my highest level of passion—I would give up my own life for their safety. In this one area, I might describe my reactions as fanatical. On all other topics, though strong opinions may exist on my part, I'm less inclined to think of myself as a fanatic, and actually think that, in the face of some new and convincing information, I would be man enough to change some of my strongly held beliefs.

What I've described here is, I believe, typical of most people. There are those, however, who are fanatical about issues and are so passionate in their defense of those beliefs that they literally are time bombs, just waiting for an innocent person to blindly stumble into the trip wire.

First of all, I guess there is nothing wrong with people feeling strongly about issues.

Second, however, for every person who believes something is absolutely right, there's always someone who thinks the very same thing is absolutely wrong.

Third, many—and maybe even most—strong beliefs are based upon less-than-full information. A true fanatic stands fast in his original belief, even in cases where he has been presented with a significant amount of new, possibly valid, but contradictory, information.

And fourth, trying to convert a fanatic to accept an opposing point of view isn't worth your time or effort.

People of opposing opinions are equally fanatical about many important issues such as religion or politics. People also become fanatical (on both sides of the fence) over issues that aren't quite some important—like baseball teams or how clean one's house has to be. Both sides of any issue can lay claim to fanatics, and both sides claim that their side is the right side.

But what does any of this have to do with the workplace environment, and why is a fanatic such a potential problem?

Clearly, there are those fanatics who would do anything in support of their beliefs, including hurting the very company they're working for if certain boundaries are crossed. I'm quite sure that some of the industrial sabotage that occurs can be laid at the doorsteps of fanatics—but probably only those fanatics who are impassioned by what we all might recognize at major issues.

I doubt that most people, in their jobs, encounter too many people who are fanatical over major issues. But fanatical supporters of what some might consider minor issues can be destructive in the workplace, too. Just say the wrong thing in their presence and watch the fur fly!

It's really interesting to watch a fanatic in a sales role, when she decides, for whatever reason, that it is her place to lecture the company's largest customer on whatever she is passionate about. Damn the torpedoes, full speed ahead! You sit there and cringe as she jumps down the throat of the customer, who has innocently stumbled into a well-concealed trap in everyday conversation. So what if the person under attack has the power to cancel the contract and move the business to your biggest competitor, it's the fanatic's issue that's important! This client has to be taught a lesson.

Often there's nothing wrong with a pointed interaction—if it's just a spirited debate, passionately argued by two opposing sides who can remain friends and colleagues after the verbal joust is over. But, oh those fanatics … for them the debate becomes personal, and we all know that everything is fair in love and war. So you are forced to sit back and watch all of your years of hard work developing this client go down the drain as the fanatic takes over with a personal attack on the poor, old, unsuspecting customer.

When dealing with a fanatic, keep the following in mind:

- If possible, find out if any fanatics work in your organization so you will know whom to avoid, or at least which topics to avoid.

- Never provoke a fanatic by intentionally bring up the counter-point to an issue in which they have a passion. While it may seem funny to you and your colleagues, it is harmful to the overall peace and stability of the working unit.

- When engaged in a conversation with a fanatic, if you hear the trip-wire trip because of what you accidentally said, be prepared to beat a hasty retreat and by all means, do not get involved in a heated conversation.

The Spy

There are two types of spies: those who are on a mission, and those who don't realize they are on a mission for someone else.

Of the spies who know they are spies, the two most obvious kinds are industrial spies and auditors. The mission of industrial spies is to infiltrate, observe, and report back. The mission of auditors is to openly enter, observe, and report back. Both of these individuals exist in the business world and we won't get into them much further in this section. I will allow that auditors are typically honest, but when everyone perceives that their mission is to uncover and report on errors, they are usually not viewed as being part of the team by many. They are viewed as interlopers whose only mission is to make people look bad, and even if you are following the rules, they always seem to find areas where you are not following the rules closely enough. In all my years, I have never seen a clean audit report. There is always something out there, some innocent mistake that provides the auditors fodder for generating unflattering reports and recommendations.

Another spy sub-group arrives abruptly and announces, "I'm here from Corporate and I'm going to help you." The word spy suggests that someone is working in the background shadows, employing stealth and cunning to avoid detection. This representative from corporate, however, frequently comes in with the brass band playing, shouting out to the world that he has arrived!

I will acknowledge that there is some harshness in my comments regarding corporate spies, so I will also acknowledge that there are those corporate representatives who truly *are* out to help you. Unfortunately, not every one is. Be that as it may, you should expect and understand that if a representative from corporate does arrive, no matter how helpful or friendly he may appear to be, he is almost always on a mission to observe and report back. What he sees and hears will be communicated back to others, so even comments and conversations that are "just between you and me," really are not—so forewarned is forearmed.

Enough said about spies who know they're spies. Let us move on to people who do not realize they are being sent on a spy mission.

It usually starts simply and seemingly innocently. Your immediate supervisor, or someone else up the food chain, calls you in and tells you that she has arranged for you to spend a few days in XYZ department for some cross training, or to get a better handle on what they do over there, or to look for ways that the two departments could better work together. "And while you're over there, make sure to talk to a lot of people—you know, to get a feel for things. Find out what they do and how they do it."

So you arrive the next day at the XYZ department, get introduced to the team, and start to observe. People answer your questions and open up to you. Before you know it, you're sharing war stories and going out to lunch together. They truly do everything they can to make you feel like part of the team, and openly share comments, ideas, problems, and suggestions, all in an effort to help make the overall organization better.

Your three-day stint in XYZ is over, and you return to report back to your boss. It's a pleasant conversation, maybe even lasting quite some time. You sense your boss is really interested. She asks you to go into great detail about the problems that XYZ is having, the new ideas that they have pending or are thinking about implementing, the comments they made about your department or your bosses—that kind of stuff. And when this meeting finally ends, you walk out, sit back down at your desk, and think all is well with the world. After all, you learned more about a different department and spent some quality time with some new colleagues. And, with the way your boss was grilling you, you must have made a good impression on her as well. Yes, all is well with the world.

Unfortunately, the person who sent you on the "training trip"—your immediate supervisor in your ABC department—hates the person running XYZ. She will use the information that you reported back not for the purpose of helping the organization, but either to make herself look better, or make the XYZ supervisor look worse. The XYZ supervisor told you they were having some problems with the new software program they are responsible for and you reported this to your boss. Later, your boss tells her boss that he'd better get prepared for bad news because XYZ is really struggling with a bunch of problems on the new software and will probably be very late in getting it to market.

The XYZ supervisor shared with you that occasionally they get late material from your ABC team, and that causes them to work faster, which unfortunately increases waste. You tell your boss, who reports to her boss that waste is way up in XYZ and we'd better find a solution: "I'll have my team get our stuff to them faster. Maybe we can help them solve their problem."

During a group lunch that you and the XYZ supervisor attended, someone told an innocent and funny story about the company president, who happened to be a personal friend from college. You report this story to your boss, who informs the president that "someone" from XYZ has been making disparaging remarks about him in public and in front of the XYZ supervisor, who did nothing to stop the comments or reprimand the individual.

Machiavellian? Yes. True? More often that it should be.

So, what lessons can we learn from this and what can we do?

Here are some statements and comments that, though not applicable 100 percent of the time, are good rules of thumb to follow:

- Not everyone from corporate is out to get you, but I would advise you that it's better to be safe then sorry. Be guarded in your comments, especially when describing problems and opinions about people. Don't lie, but if you don't need to say something, don't.

- An auditor's mission is to keep digging until he finds something. Most audits encompass a wide enough scope that sooner or later something will be uncovered: some mistake in procedure, approval level, or a proper signature in the proper place. I once had a controller who told me that he purposefully let some small mistakes exist in the books, like an unsigned reimbursed business expense form, so the auditors could "find" something and stop looking. He did this because he had recorded some accruals on the books that he didn't want challenged. Unfortunately, I didn't insist he do things right. I figured he knew the world of finance better than I did so I let him have his way. Eventually, his loosey-goosey accounting practices cost me my job!

- Not everyone coming into your department to work on a project or to undergo training is someone else's covert spy … but anyone might be. Make sure you establish a relationship with these people and get to know them before you open up. Find out who their management chain-of-command is and try to find out if any of them are out to gain points at the expense of your department.

- When you are asked to visit another department and report on their activities, by all means do as you're told, but be cognizant that other factors may be at work here. Be circumspect in what you report back and how you report it. What you say or write could be used against others.

The Boss

Listing your boss in the "to-be-avoided-if-you-can" category may sound a bit incongruous. After all, he is your boss. How can you avoid him? Better yet, why would you want to avoid him?

We said previously that bosses have three general roles:

1. To be the leader who sets examples and, through his actions, encourages others to follow and excel

2. To be the coach who strives to keep the team performing at excellent levels by motivating them and providing the tools and support needed to succeed

3. To be the boss, ensuring that rules, regulations, policies, and procedures are met, and applying a well-aimed kick to the seat of the pants when anyone is caught straying from the path

But what about the bad boss? What makes him bad? And why do organizations have and tolerate bad bosses?

What makes some bosses bad include:

- They shouldn't have been promoted in the first place; the water's just too deep for them. The flesh is willing but the skill set falls short.

- They are burned out and, as a direct result, they just don't care anymore.

- They lack the training necessary to be an effective boss. The raw skill set necessary that makes a good supervisor does not exist within every individual. In some cases, people are promoted into higher-level roles and are just expected to flourish automatically or "figure it out."

- They lack the respect of the people they are charged with managing; thus, no matter what they do or how they do it, they are perceived as bad.

- They have the skill set and training, but not the personality or disposition.

Signs that you are working for a bad boss include:

- Your boss is unable or unwilling to provide you with meaningful comments, suggestions, and constructive criticism.

- Your boss relies solely on one of the three basic roles to address every situation (leader, coach or policeman).

  o A bad boss can give the appearance of leading. She can spout all of the worn and tired clichés, believing that she is truly leading and motivating. Yet her actions clearly demonstrate her own inability or unwillingness to actually use those approaches as guides for her own actions. As the worn and tired cliché points out, she can "talk the talk," but she can't "walk the talk."

  o A bad boss can give the appearance of coaching: it's easy to continually use slogans and encouraging words to motivate others, thus avoiding having to do some real, thoughtful work that will solve some real issues.

o A bad boss is an overly aggressive policeman, constantly in search of procedural crimes: "You work while I sit back and criticize your every mistake."

- No matter how hard he tries, your bad boss's crappy personality just makes you want to turn and run away.

The reasons that organizations tolerate these bad bosses, at least for longer than they should, starts with the reasons why people become bad bosses, which are identical to the reasons that people become empty suits:

- An employee is promoted to or above the individual's Peter Principle level.

- An employee is transferred based upon seniority or past job performance into a completely new area (for example, the sales manager is given the role of accounting department manager).

- An event leads to a personal breakdown, which may not have any other outward signs other than the empty suit syndrome.

- An employee is protected by a sponsor who is unable or unwilling to recognize the employee's many shortcomings.

- An employee makes a conscious decision to rest on her past laurels and milk the system.

Some bad bosses are so obviously bad that their tenure as boss has to be cut short before the organization starts to pay dearly for the original mistake of promoting them in the first place. Other bad bosses, however, have a way of blending into the organizational background sufficiently so that just the people who report directly to them realize how bad they truly are.

Bad bosses frequently employ the following forms of camouflage, all designed to mask their ineptitude:

- They surround themselves with good people.

- They claim the credit when something good happens, but avoid the responsibility for errors and mistakes.

- They never expose their direct reports to their own bosses, thus becoming communication funnels for the information flow.

- They always ask a direct report to handle the preparation of presentations, proposals, speeches, and reports that they then pass off as their own original work.

- They avoid direct answers to difficult questions.

Organizations tolerate, or at least appear to tolerate, the bad boss because:

- Those above the bad boss really do not see her shortcomings. The department's results are acceptable; therefore it is logical to assume that the boss must be doing a good job as well.

- The bad boss has done a good job in preparing his immediate supervisor. He has made the case that there are rabble-rousers in the group who may make some disparaging remarks about him. So when rumors about Joe being a bad boss start to surface, those making the complaints are simply viewed as being disloyal or as the troublemakers who probably are not doing their job right.

- The bad boss is being protected:

  o By the person who promoted him and who does not want to publicly admit to the original error of the promotion.

  o By the company's culture. The person at the top of the pyramid really does not care how the manager treats people or how she performs. All he cares about are the results. Good results always hide a lot of problems in this type of company. (NOTE: Many companies have adopted 360° performance reviews in an effort to make sure communications and evaluations flow both up and down their organizational structure. When this system works as designed, it is difficult for the bad boss to hide behind his or her employees.)

- The bad boss claims all of the credit for the group's successes, and assigns blame for all of the failures, therefore casting himself in the best light possible.

So, we know what makes a good boss, and we know what makes a bad boss—and what types of behavior they both exhibit. And we even know why organizations tolerate bad bosses. Only one real question remains: How can you avoid a bad boss?

Well, you can't avoid him in the traditional sense of simply not coming into contact with him, or interacting with him. After all, he is your boss. So, in order to make sure you can survive this situation you might consider using the following approaches:

- Always be pleasant to the boss, no matter how much of a jerk she may be. The last thing you need to do is to give her fuel for the fire—the fire she will attempt to throw you in as matters escalate within the organization.

- If possible, always have an additional member of the team attend any meetings or interactions of substance you have with your boss. A witness sometimes proves very useful in the he-said-she-said reviews that frequently occur when all hell breaks loose.

- Document everything of substance. If you are preparing the letters, memos, presentations, and/or speeches for your boss, make sure you submit each one with a cover letter indicating what you have done for her. And since we live in an electronic world, it's easy keep all draft and final copies of your labors, which could be used to demonstrate your contributions in the event that push comes to shove.

- If you are able to develop a good working relationship with a bad boss (tough if you are trying to avoid him … but it could happen) and he is truly interested in improving his managerial skills, assist him in his development. It may not make any difference in the long run to his ability to manage better, but it could provide you with some protection if, and probably when, the boss decides to come looking for someone's head to chop off.

- Recognize that in today's fast-paced world, where the only constant is the increasing rate of change, no one boss will stay in her position forever, so having patience can help.

The Customer

The vast majority of my career has been spent in various sales roles, including sales representative, major account manager, regional sales manager, vice present of sales, senior vice president of sales and marketing, and president of a sales corporation subsidiary. In all my positions, from my first position as an estimator to my last position as a group president of a business unit, I found myself in regular, numerous interactions with customers and prospective customers. And now that I have my own business, I realize more than ever before that without customers, my business would not exist. So, customers are supremely important to any business whose mission is to produce a product or provide a service that a customer is going to purchase.

Obviously, but easily forgotten at times.

When someone in a company decides to place an order for a product or a service from another company, that decision is often based, at least in part, upon the relationship that has developed between the people involved in the buying and selling processes. The customer-company's representatives (purchasing agents, procurement staff, users of the products or services) form both personal and business bonds with representatives from the seller-company's organization (sales people, production teams, quality assurance personnel).

This point is a little less obvious, but still fairly understandable.

Often, the relationship that exists between the two companies is based upon the strength of the relationship between two main people: the buyer and the sales representative. In any given situation, it may be people at different levels of either organization, say the CEO of one firm and the VP of another, but typically, there is one relationship between two key people that is truly the strongest. For this section, we will discuss only the basic main buyer/sales representative relationship.

So, the stage is set. Company ABC agrees to purchase some products or a list of services from company XYZ. The ABC representative, Mike, and the XYZ representative, Joan, hit it off pretty well and they do a good job representing their respective companies in the negotiations. Along the way, the professional relationship grows and they become pretty good friends as well.

Over time, as with most of these relationships, one or both of the parties ends up with a different assignment, maybe even at a different firm, and a new person is introduced into the buy/sell equation. This relationship may or may not develop in a mutually positive way. In one case, I was the seventh or eighth sales person assigned to a major account, where I met Ziggy.

In The Good section of this book, I introduced you to Ziggy, who became a close friend. Ziggy had been pushing his boss for more responsibilities, which meant more prestige and a bigger paycheck. He got it, but with a quid-pro-quo attached. There almost always is a quid-pro-quo somewhere in there.

If Ziggy's job was going to be expanded, his boss told him that he was going to have to take Wally into his group. Now, Wally was a blend of 50 percent empty suit, 30 percent obnoxious and 20 percent just plain crappy personality. He simply could not fit in with or play nicely with others. He had been bounced around the organization for over twenty years as boss after boss failed to deal with the situation, each one using a transfer as a convenient way of ridding themselves of the problem child. Now Ziggy really wanted that promotion, so he agreed to accept Wally, the problem child. And where do you think Ziggy put Wally so he wouldn't disrupt the rest of his organization?

You're right! He became the main customer interface assigned to work closely with the main supplier interface—me!

Well, I'm here to tell you that this association with Wally started my four-and-a-half-year journey through salesman's hell. This guy was a real piece of work. Here is just a brief list of the kinds of things he did to drive my organization, his organization, and me crazy:

- First and foremost, he really believed that the customer is always right. There are some areas where the customer may always be right, like their expectations and their specifications. But he literally felt that he was right in everything, including his views and opinions on business in general, religion, politics, and sports. At first we all thought he was kidding. Much to our amazement, he actually thought he was right, which not only led to some very convoluted and confusing discussions over the years, but also resulted in much pain and aggravation for me as he phoned my boss to complain about my views on this or that, all of which were totally unrelated to the job at hand.

- As soon as you believe you're always right, you've closed the door on negotiations. Much of the business between our two companies was based on the give-and-take of negotiations, like agreeing to mutually acceptable production schedules for the next year. Wally would not have any part of it. He wanted his schedules, without changes and without any of the extra costs associated with his unreasonable demands.

- Good sales people sometimes ask a customer or prospect to bring their spouse or significant other along to a dinner or special event—it helps cement the bond between the sales person and the customer/prospect. One day Wally asked me if it was okay to bring his wife. Obviously, I said, "Yes," and actually felt embarrassed that I hadn't offered before. She became a permanent fixture at the dinners we had from then on. He also had many children, who from time to time joined in as well. Now this would not necessarily have been bad if the relationship between Wally and me had been strong. But, since it was Wally, those evenings quickly became personal glimpses of hell on earth.

- Wally would invite me over to his house for drinks and conversation. We would go out together to buy some beer, and pick up another twenty or thirty dollars of everything and anything from nuts and popcorn to hamburgers and hotdogs. The first time this happened, it seemed like a great idea—beer and some munchies, followed by a grilled hot dog or two. But I got only the beer. He never offered me any of the other stuff. This became a monthly ritual—going to the store with him, buying a bunch of stuff, and ending up with only a beer.

- Then came the day when we toured the plant of one of the raw material suppliers we used. After the tour, the company representative generously offered each of us a sweater embroidered with his company's name and logo. Wally said, "Thanks! You know, my kids would really like one of these, could I have six more?"

- Throughout the years I had various meeting with Wally in his office. When it came to lunchtime, we'd always try and gather up a few more people from his company to join us. Almost every time, everyone was too busy to have lunch with us. But if I visited the office when Wally was on vacation, or on a business trip, I'd practically have to rent a bus to get all the volunteers out to lunch. As long as Wally wasn't around, people wanted to spend time with me. When he was there … well, they were busy.

I could go on and on with Wally stories, but I won't.

Sometimes you end up with a primary contact in the customer's organization who ends up being a real pain in the butt. What do you do?

Here are some strategies and tactics you will want to consider:

- Since you have to deal with your own Wally, find out as much as you can about him so you can put his comments and actions in perspective. He may be difficult because he is unsure how to handle the power, authority, and responsibility he has. He may be unsure how to act and when to make demands as opposed to asking politely. So, establishing the best relationship possible between the two of you will be the first step.

- This person may be insecure. Helping your Wally achieve some "wins," whatever they may be, can help break the ice and bring him back to even keel. I'm not advocating doing anything that will materially hurt your side of the business, but agreeing to go to the ABC restaurant for the fifteenth time because he likes the place isn't that big of a sacrifice. On the job, if he asks for some minor concession, give in. Sometimes, he just needs a win.

- Make sure you expand your network of contacts within Wally's organization. Get to know his boss, other people in the department, and people in different departments. This way, you will establish your own set of relationships with these people so they can form their own opinion of you and the work you're doing on their behalf—and not simply have to rely on Wally's view of the world.

- Document everything that occurs with Wally. If he makes you agree to something that is risky or flat-out wrong, it will come in handy when you can produce the letter that says you did what you did because he ordered you to do it. Obviously, these types of documents need to be tactfully written, but it's really worth the time and effort.

- Make sure you tell your colleagues about Wally and his eccentricities. You don't want someone in your organization coming unglued when exposed to him for the first time. And by all means make sure your boss meets Wally and has a clear understanding about his persona. It will help you down the road should Wally start complaining about the bad job you're doing.

THE UGLY

People you will want to avoid at all costs

The Owner

Every business has a boss—someone in charge of the strategic direction of the enterprise. Under this boss are a variety of sub-bosses. Depending upon the size of the company, there may be numerous levels of bosses, from the lower levels such as supervisors and department managers, up to the executive levels such as senior vice presidents, division presidents, COOs, CIOs, CEOs, vice-chairman of the board, and board chairs.

In many companies, there is also the position of owner—the ultimate boss. The owner may not have that particular title on a business card, though some actually do. But this person is the original entrepreneur who decided to invest the time, energy, and money required to start a business. Some of these efforts result in small businesses that have fewer than five employees—in some cases only the owner. Other times, the business grows and become huge, employing thousands of people.

First of all, I have nothing against entrepreneurs. Heck, I am one!

Second, we all have admiration for people who venture out on their own and start a business because they feel that they will succeed. After all, few of us start anything with the intention of having it become a complete and utter failure.

Third, very few entrepreneurs, or owners, become candidates for The Ugly category.

So, with these caveats in place, let us proceed.

Owners typically can strike it big from a financial perspective in one of three ways: the business is successful and through that success the business generates significant profits; the business, which may or may not be profitable, is sold and the owner hits the big payday through the buy-out; or the business is profitable and it goes public, with the owner keeping a large block of stock that can generate capital gains and dividends in addition to the actual value of the stock itself.

During my career, I've encountered all three situations. The two largest companies I worked for were publicly held companies that had their origins as privately held companies owned either by the person who started the business in the first place, or the original owner's heirs. I was also involved in a couple of acquisitions of family-owned businesses, and I am now the owner of my own business.

After the entrepreneur starts up the business and attains some level of market acceptance, it is quite normal that additional workers are required to handle the growth. And after a while, if the business growth continues, more and more internal infrastructure growth occurs as well. When Tom first started the business, he used an outside attorney to handle his legal affairs and an outside firm to handle the taxes. His wife Betty took care of the bookkeeping while Tom handled sales, marketing, purchasing, manufacturing, and customer service. As more and more people began ordering his widgets, he added a customer service person to handle the coordination of orders with the growing customer base. Before long, he had to add a couple of people to help him manufacture the widgets. Then he added someone to help in the selling effort. At the end of the year the bookkeeping chores grew too complex for Betty to handle alone so he hired an accountant, who also could handle the year-end tax preparation. Five years later, Tom employed over 350 people including Betty, their two sons, and one daughter. Fifteen years later, Tom retired and left the business to his children. Then, three years after that, the kids decided they didn't really give a hoot about making widgets for the rest of their lives and decided to sell the business. Sometimes a company like this stays in the family for several generations but, more often than not, if the business is successful, it will eventually go public or be sold outright.

Probably the worst individual in the owner category is the owner who sells the business—either through a public stock sale or to another owner—but stays in place to run the business. Even though the person is no longer the 100 percent owner, she continues to operate as if she does have full ownership. Some used-to-be-owners finding themselves in this position continue to act exactly the same way they did when they did have full ownership. So what? Why is this necessarily bad?

When you are the full, 100 percent owner of a business, the business is yours. You are completely entitled to do what you think is right even if everyone else thinks it's wrong. Once you share the company with other owners, you should take everyone's thoughts, opinions and perspectives into consideration. And if you're simply the largest shareholder in a publicly held company, you should recognize the fact that you are just one of the shareholders, even if you're the largest shareholder. Using your majority stock ownership position as an excuse to ignore basic common decency as well as the thoughts and opinions of the other owners and members of the organization is flat-out wrong.

The other issue that flows directly out of this situation is the fact that the owner has most likely hired many capable people—people who expect that their opinions, ideas, and decisions will be supported by the boss (owner). Very often these employees become frustrated when the owner pulls rank and makes decisions for them time after time, or never accepting their recommendations. In all cases the owner is blind to her actions and impact on others, or when the situation is brought to her attention, she very often responds by saying, "Hey, remember, it's my company."

When dealing with the owner, make sure you remember that:

- She is the owner and she is entitled to get her way.

- The enterprise is the owner's baby. Criticizing the enterprise is criticizing the owner.

- Owners are people and people have flaws. Help the owner in those areas where he might need some assistance in character refinement, but do so in a way that doesn't force him into the role of owner. Most people do appreciate help and will respond well to constructive criticism if handled in the right manner.

The Owner's Kid

Quite a few second- and third-generation owners are decent people. Others, instead of being born with that proverbial silver spoon in their mouths, may seem to have that utensil lodged in another, less attractive orifice, if their spoiled brat behavior is any indication. They think that simply because Mom or Dad made it big in business and passed along the reins to them, they, too, are capable of great things. In fact, many of them think they're even more capable than their sires and are hell-bent on a mission to prove just how smart they think they really are.

I like to refer to these types of generational owners as Mr. and Ms. Pileadough. They have a pile of money and the only real claim they have to it is that the stork stopped at the right house at the right time. These individuals grow up in the lap of luxury, with parents or grandparents who made it big. Starting from birth, they have been exposed to piles of dough, nice homes, great vacations, and shiny new sports cars on their sixteenth birthdays, box seats on the fifty-yard line—ad nauseam.

We have all encountered the spoiled and snotty rich kid—the one who goes through money like someone else is earning it, the one who has everything, including an opinion about everything and everyone, and just happens to know everything. Now, sit back and imagine this person is your boss, either directly or somewhere else in the chain of command!

The bad characteristics of the owner's kid include:

- Complete and utter disregard for employees, whom he truly views as assets to be acquired, used, and ultimately discarded

- Frequent negative comments about all of the mistakes made by the original founder of the business

- The need to surround herself with sycophants, and then to empower them, which wreaks further havoc on the working environment

- The need to take credit for all of the successes and seek scapegoats for all of the failures

- The inability to accept the fact that he made a mistake ("It wasn't my plan that was bad, it was your execution,") and that can lead to your (figurative) "execution"!

- An inability to articulate a clear and compelling vision for the enterprise ... to simply "make it bigger" does not cut it when you are supposed to be the leader.

Here are a few suggestions that may go a long way in helping you to cope with this type of situation should you ever work for your own Pileadough:

- First of all, remember that no matter how close you may feel your relationship is with these characters, they have the ability, much like chameleons, to change right before your eyes. Pileadough types never, ever forget that they are the owners and that employees are simple assets of their companies.

- Second, never expect these individuals to admit they are wrong. Oh, they may say that they are wrong, but they will immediately look for the person or persons who gave them the "bad advice", "didn't deliver on the commitment", or "overestimated the market's potential". The Pileadough types make the wrong decisions and make the mistakes but someone else—anyone else—ends up paying the price.

- Finally, make sure you keep your network active and your resume up to date. Working in this type of environment is grueling and even if you are lucky enough to avoid getting fired, you will find little if any joy working under this type of owner.

On a sidebar note, these second- and third-generation owners are often referred to as being real SOBs, which apparently means son of boss ... or does it?

The Fast-Tracker

There are two types of fast-trackers: The first type is the individual who is truly a great performer and, because of performance on the job, is given all the support and training necessary to continue a rapid rise up the corporate ladder. This is the individual who is admired by virtually everyone because of her contributions to the overall effort and is well liked and a pleasure to be around. The second type is the opinionated loudmouth who bursts on the scene and announces that she is the chosen one, some fair-haired, soon-to-be next president of the company. We will explore the personality of the second type, as the first type is definitely not a member of the Ugly persuasion.

First, we need to understand who the ugly fast-tracker typically is—most likely one of the following:

- A relative or close personal friend of the founder of the company

- A relative or close personal friend of a senior-level executive such as the chairperson, CEO, CFO, or COO

- A relative or close personal friend of an influential customer or supplier

- A relative or close personal friend of a local, regional, state, or national politician who possesses a great deal of clout

We could list more but I believe you get the idea. The ugly fast-tracker usually isn't John or Jane Doe who walked into the human resources department and asked to fill out an application. (Actually, John or Jane might turn out to be a good fast-tracker).

So the ugly fast-tracker starts out with a huge chip on her shoulder. Why? Because she is someone who knows someone. Her old man and the president were fraternity brothers, or her Uncle Bill is the chairman, or her brother's the mayor.

Now I'm not saying that these individuals may not be capable in terms of skills and abilities. Some are quite smart and can make important contributions to the company. What I am saying is that, in many cases, these individuals are not major contributors to the effort and, on top of that, they are just plain obnoxious. They strut around as if they're God's gift to the world, not relying on their contributions to garner respect, but demanding respect because they know someone. They treat peers and subordinates as rungs on the corporate ladder and step on these people repeatedly. They are not shy about telling you that they are destined for great things, nor are they shy about telling you what things will be like when they take over. They seem to have an answer for every question (many of which are wrong), and have an opinion about everything, which they are also not shy about sharing. They can see everyone else's mistakes, yet are blind to their own shortcomings.

If the only problem with ugly fast-trackers were their own obnoxiousness, we might be able to stomach them for a while. And one nice thing about fast-trackers is that they come and go rather quickly. If you're able to avoid getting caught under their feet as they run through the position learning the ropes, count yourself lucky.

One of the biggest downsides about ugly fast-trackers is that they really do know someone—Uncle Bill really is the chairman. And because they are connected, and feel the continuous urge to appear in the know, they frequently pontificate at the expense of others. You get one of these jerks mad and, all of a sudden, the chairman is hearing from his favorite niece about you, and in a not too flattering a way.

So, like the gatekeeper personality who "protects" a purchasing agent from a sales person, an ugly fast-tracker might not be able to do you any good, but it is potentially very easy for her to do you some real harm. So, forewarned is forearmed.

As far as strategies for dealing with the ugly fast-tracker, you might consider the following:

- Be cautious in both word and action around fast-trackers and make certain you don't provide them with any ammunition that they could use against you at a later time.

- Document your dealings, when appropriate, to keep a paper trail of who really came up with the brilliant idea or solved the unsolvable problem will help you get the recognition you may rightly deserve.

- When practical, avoid one-on-one meetings. Having someone else along can prevent the possibility of future, no-win I-said-you-said battles.

The Hatchet Man

Like the bounty hunters of the old west, the hatchet man (or hatchet woman!) rides into your life, as well as the lives of many others, causing pain, anguish, and death—at least in terms of your career.

These people are noted for their ability to completely and utterly disregard the feelings of others as they move through a team, department, division, or company, whacking people left and right. They are on a holy mission to reduce costs, get rid of the old regime, or bring in new blood. They have the full support of those who sent them, so you don't have the traditional recourse of appealing to a higher authority.

Typically, a hatchet "person" isn't required when the employee is being axed due to performance issues. That's what bosses and HR professionals are for. No, the hatchet man appears when there is no good reason to get rid of people other than the fact that someone else, at a higher level, feels that they need to be removed. And the appearance of the hatchet man is also usually reserved for multiple firings—like the closing of a department or the downsizing of a division.

We won't spend any time discussing the personality traits of the hatchet man, since knowing these would not help you avoid or confront him. At the end of the day, suffice it to say that these people usually seem to like what they do, and they tend to do a good job of making others miserable. Since they wield power, they are feared and disliked as they go about their business.

There really are not any strategies available to avoid or even hide from the hatchet man once his mission has been defined. If you happen to be working in a department that's slated to be closed, that's just the luck of the draw. If your performance to date has been great, you may be one of the few lucky ones to receive a transfer to another area of the company. However, if you are just average, or a poor performer, or not connected to anyone in power, you will not succeed in your quest to stay employed. You may miss the ax the first time around by making a stink about discrimination, or calling in an old marker from someone on high but, eventually, if you are on the list to be axed, your head will hit the ground.

So, in the face of this story of doom and gloom, what should you do?

People speak of situational awareness—being in tune with what is going on around you. This is an excellent place to start. You should know what is happening within your work group, your department, your division, and the enterprise at large. You should be aware of your own level of performance and your personal contribution to the good of the enterprise. You should strive to achieve the highest levels of performance. And if and when you start to see signs of trouble, seek out the counsel of a coach or mentor who can help you assess the situation and develop a plan of action.

Now most of us, as individuals, cannot typically impact our organizations to a great degree. Sure, you can make the huge mistake or make the big sale, but by and large, your efforts are just one building block in the wall that supports the company. So, the only course of action that makes sense is to strive to do a good job and stay informed about everything going on around you. In this way, you may be saved because of your performance record, or at least be in a position to see that the future is not rosy and that you should start considering working elsewhere.

This is also a great opportunity to interject that you should always have an updated resume available and that you should update it at least twice a year. Further, remember that both your formal and informal networks may provide you with valuable support and assistance if you elect (or are forced) to look for a new job.

The Customer

No one loves a customer more than the sales person assigned to the account. It stands to reason that the customer may be sole purpose for the sales person's existence. Without the customer, the organization would not need the sales person. Of course without customers, the organization would not need anyone at all!

Sales people exist because there are customers who need things—and customers who <u>think</u> they need things exist because there are salespeople. I believe this is a fundamental fact of business. But then again, the majority of my career has been in sales, so take this passionately stated fundamental fact with a grain of salt.

In The Good section, I introduced you to Ziggy. In The Bad section, I introduced you to Wally. In this section, we will see what happened when Wally transitioned from Bad Customer to Ugly Customer.

Wally was bad because of a combination of his personality, his lack of understanding about what his job was really all about (often referred to as the empty suit syndrome), and his innate ability to simply be obnoxious. He was difficult to stomach, and dealing with him was a pain in the neck, but, what the heck, he was a customer, he essentially paid my commissions, and for my own benefit, I endured his personality.

In an attempt to increase their revenues, the company Wally worked for introduced a new product, and though it was somewhat similar to the product that my company was already producing for him at the time, it was different.

The company that I worked for also produced the new product line that Wally wanted to purchase, but he felt that he would do his company a favor by expanding the search for possible suppliers beyond the two or three providers he normally called upon for bids and proposals. Lo and behold, after several months of searching for a supplier, going through the regular requests for information, requests for quotations, quotation reviews, and the final selection process, Wally recommended to his superiors that they award the business to a competitor of mine rather than accept my proposal. At the time, Wally probably made the right recommendation based upon a comparison of the economics. I reported the news to my chain of command. My chain of command reported the loss to the side of the business that would have actually been involved in producing this new product line on behalf of Wally's company. Their chain of command berated my chain of command, saying they should have had of one their own sales people selling their services rather than relying on me. Obviously, my chain of command could not argue back since I had, in fact, lost the opportunity, and I quickly found myself in the corporate doghouse.

As far as I was concerned, Wally had declared war on me. By not awarding me the new business, he had eliminated a commission opportunity for me and he made me look bad in the process, which in the corporate environment is a serious issue. I was determined to rectify this situation and—long story short—I was able to convince Wally's chain of command that Wally made a mistake in recommending my competition. In fact, the letter of intent that was issued to the competition was withdrawn and my company was eventually awarded the contract.

And with that award, I went from the corporate doghouse to the winner's circle, all in about two weeks worth of hard-charging, behind-the-scenes selling on my part. Yet even this happy ending had a devastating impact on my relationship with Wally, because Wally suddenly felt he had become the victim of a personal attack—he looked bad in front of his chain of command. Right before my very eyes, Wally morphed from Bad Customer into Ugly Customer.

All of a sudden I could not do anything right in Wally's eyes. Even when I did exactly what he wanted, it either wasn't fast enough, big enough, or small enough.

I will be the first to admit that I created this monster and stepped into the jaws of the trap all by myself. I failed to make the sale in the first place, though to this day I submit that Wally's goal was to simply bring in a second supplier. I failed to consider how a reversal of the letter of intent would reflect on Wally, and I did not go out of my way to suck up to him after I was able to get his chain of command to reverse their decision. Wally never forgave me, even after I was able to demonstrate that the company he had selected could not possibly have fulfilled their obligations. He did everything in his power to hurt my career. Almost everyone else realized what he was up to and ignored him. In the last six months of his career, just before he retired, I got a new boss, one who unfortunately fell into The Ugly category. All this jerk needed to hear from a customer was how bad I was. Well, one thing led to another and I was faced with the choice of accepting an unearned demotion or resigning. I resigned.

Not all ugly customers are created by sales people. Here are some situations that can turn a customer ugly:

- He is told that he is too lax with the suppliers and has been taken advantage of—so he overreacts and becomes ugly.

- She has never been a buyer before and doesn't realize she might benefit by playing by the rules of engagement established by the previous buyer.

- He is a recent outside hire that has been brought in to "shake things up a bit".

- She resents the fact that you replaced her favorite sales person by getting promoted or transferred into the sales position.

- He simply has a crappy personality and possesses no interpersonal skills.

As far as handling the Ugly customer, consider these suggestions:

- In the case of a new buyer, understand her individual needs and expectations instead of simply employing strategies and tactics that worked successfully with her predecessor.

- Make a true and concerted effort to establish rapport.

- Make sure your chain of command is exposed to him so that they have an appreciation of the situation facing you.

- Document all interactions with the customer to avoid ambiguities, and provide a paper trail in case the fur begins to fly when things don't go well.

The Two-Faced

The two-faced individual may very well be the ugliest of the ugly characters. And it is the absolute worst case possible when the two-faced individual happens to be your boss, or someone else relatively close to you but above you in the chain of command. First, let us look at the characteristics of the two-faced individual:

- He always has a hidden agenda.

- She changes masks at the drop of a hat whenever doing so will be to her advantage.

- He hides his true persona from his superiors.

- She manipulates, uses, and abuses people for the sole purpose of improving her own position.

- He uses the comments of others, even those shared under confidence, out of context in his attacks on individuals.

- When challenged, she offers a seemingly reasonable explanation (that masks her true intentions) for her two-faced behavior.

- He somehow is always able to come away from a bad situation smelling like a rose.

A two-faced individual who is a peer would do something like the following:

- You mention that the volume of projects you are working on is so large that you are concerned you may not have enough time to do what's necessary to complete the projects on time. The two-faced individual tells your mutual boss to check your work closely for errors and omissions because you mentioned that you didn't have time to do your work adequately and on time.

- You mention that even though you're quite busy, you have to take some time off to take your child to the doctor. The two-faced individual mentions to your mutual boss that you left work early for no apparent reason, despite the fact that you haven't finished an assigned project.

- You mention that while on a trip with the boss, both of you had a few drinks and had a good time. The two-faced individual tells others that you said the boss has a drinking problem.

Scary? You'd better believe it. An exaggeration? Not at all.

Why? Because most of the time you don't know that the individual you are dealing with is two-faced and you certainly don't know what they are saying about you behind your back. These fiends are very capable when it comes to protecting their identity. They use subterfuge and confusion to mask their true identities until the damage is done, and then it is too late. And even then you may not have a clue as to who sold you down the river. The motivation behind their actions is usually that they see you as either an immediate threat or a future threat.

The two-faced individual is a master at deflecting blame onto someone else that should rightly be placed at her own doorstep. She poisons the well by slowly and deliberately letting someone else know that she has suspicions about you. At first, she appears to accuse you of something, using someone else's words. But then she seems to jump to your defense. I've heard people say, "Roger can't be trusted, but I've never personally witnessed any deceit on his part." Or, "Sally must be really smart. She seems to get her work done in half the time it takes everyone else, which gives her a lot of time to kibitz around the water cooler."

These people plant the seeds of your destruction, fertilizing them from time to time with some innocent, yet tasty, bit of BS, hoping for germination. Not every seed planted will germinate, and even if one does it does not necessarily mean the end of your career. However, if the people in charge hear enough of these unfounded accusations against you, or even hear only one at the wrong time, you may not get the promotion, be assigned to the big project, or be tapped for further development within the organization. The two-faced individual, as a peer, can truly hurt you.

A harsh picture? Not really. This stuff happens every day, day in and day out. And the larger the organization you work for, the greater the chance that you will eventually encounter a two-faced individual.

But as bad a dream as having a two-faced individual as a co-worker might be, here is the real nightmare scenario—the two-faced individual becomes your boss, or your bosses' boss. The price of poker just went up.

If for whatever reason the two-faced boss decides he doesn't like you, you are doomed. He can and will find a way to make your life miserable. And here is how he can accomplish that:

- First, he asks you what is going on in your area of responsibility. You give him an honest appraisal of what's happening. You tell him all about the projects you are working on, the status, and the challenges, if any.

- Second, he asks whether you've considered doing a particular task in this manner or in that manner. You answer accordingly—either you did or you didn't.

- Third, he asks whether you need assistance. Again, you answer accordingly.

Seems innocent enough, does it not?

Here is how the two-faced boss spins your answers:

- First, he asks you what is going on in your area of responsibility.

  o You leave out some details and he spins your answers to suggest that you are trying to hide problems.

- o You don't leave out any details and he spins that to suggest you don't have enough to do and that you're just coasting through with your assignments with nominal effort.

- Second, he asks whether you've considered doing a particular task in this manner or in that manner.

  - o You answer, "Yes, I've tried that," and he spins that answer to suggest that you rejected advice from the boss.

  - o You answer, "No, I haven't tried that," and he spins that to suggest that you have limited vision and are not a creative thinker.

- Third, he asks whether you need assistance.

  - o You answer, "Yes, I could use some help," and he spins that to suggest you are overwhelmed and can't handle your assignments.

  - o You answer, "No, thanks, I don't need any assistance," and he spins that to suggest you're not being a team player.

Fortunately, there are not too many two-faced bosses out there, but there are a few, so beware. If you get on their wrong side, they will set you up for the fall. Here's one way that this could by made to happen.

Your new, two-faced boss just had his initial three-question meeting with you and the other members of his new group. Then he meets with his boss, who asks, "So, what do you think about your new team?"

The two-faced boss quickly dons the mask of the concerned, organization-oriented manager and says, "Overall, they seem to be a pretty decent bunch, but there are some problems that concern me. For example, I made a few suggestions to Jack about the project he was working on and he didn't want to even consider trying them. He simply rejected them out of hand. Seems to be fairly close-minded. Joan may not be the team player we all thought she was. I offered her some help from others and she quickly said she didn't need any help. Might be hiding some problems. I asked Josh how things were going on his end and he never mentioned the problem he had with the accounting department. Sounded like he was trying to cover something up. Of course, this is only my first day here, but it appears we may need to make some changes. I'm not prepared to recommend anything right now. Give me a few more weeks to sniff around and I'll give you a plan of action as to how we can shake things up and drive some improvements to the bottom line."

The boss of the two-faced individual walks away from the meeting feeling that he has a hard-charger running the department now and that things are in good hands. The two-faced individual walks away from the meeting knowing that he planted some great seeds, once again donning his ugly mask—and knowing full well that, once again, he has fooled the boss.

A couple of weeks later, if Jack, Joan, and Josh complain to the boss's boss about the behavior or unfairness of their two-faced boss, the big boss is already predisposed to believe that they are simply poor performers who are making disparaging remarks about their boss just to keep their jobs. And the vicious cycle repeats itself.

If you end up with a two-faced boss you might consider using the following approaches, which are the same strategies to use if you have a bad boss:

- Always be pleasant to the boss, no matter how much of a jerk she may be. The last thing you need to do is to give her fuel for the fire—the fire she will attempt to throw you in as matters escalate within the organization.

- If possible, always have an additional member of the team attend any meetings or interactions of substance you have with your boss. A witness sometimes proves very useful in the he-said-she-said reviews that frequently occur when all hell breaks loose.

- Document everything of substance. If you are preparing the letters, memos, presentations, and/or speeches for your boss, make sure you submit each one with a cover letter indicating what you have done for her. And since we live in an electronic world, it's easy keep all draft and final copies of your labors, which could be used to demonstrate your contributions in the event that push comes to shove.

- If you are able to develop a good working relationship with a bad boss (tough if you are trying to avoid him … but it could happen) and he is truly interested in improving his managerial skills, assist him in his development. It may not make any difference in the long run to his ability to manage better, but it could provide you with some protection if, and probably when, the boss decides to come looking for someone's head to chop off.

- Recognize that in today's fast-paced world, where the only constant is the increasing rate of change, no one boss will stay in her position forever, so having patience can help.

A good working relationship with a two-faced boss may be tough to develop, especially if you are trying to avoid contact, but it could provide you with some protection if, and probably when, the boss decides to come looking for someone's head.

THE
CHARACTERS
IN REVIEW

Summary comments worth remembering

THE GOOD

The Co-Worker Who Starts on the Same Day

Most people you meet for the first time under non-threatening circumstances exhibit the following characteristics:

- They feel comfortable to be relatively open, honest, and pleasant in their communications with you.

- They do not have preconceived notions of wants and needs relative to their interaction with you.

- They engage in conversations covering a variety of topics.

- They are able to disagree with you on a point or topic without becoming belligerent in their communications style.

The Friend

- They have somewhat similar likes and dislikes to yours.

- They are able to communicate effectively with you.

- They are able to disagree with you on a topic or point without becoming belligerent.

- They are supportive of your needs and desires, and attempt to help you achieve them when their attainment is practical.

- They come to your aid in times of need.

The Potential Network Member

- They display the willingness to become part of a network.

- They provide the type of assistance necessary to become an integral part of your network.

- They provide you with new perspectives on issues, problems, and challenges, and do so in a way that is both constructive and positive.

The Smart One

- They have the ability to tackle difficult issues and situations.

- They have the same personality quirks as anyone else, though they may be a bit more pronounced.

- They possess a willingness to help others though they may not always possess the patience to explain things thoroughly to others.

- They may have a caustic or dry sense of humor that makes them appear aloof.

The Team Member

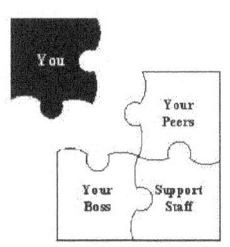

- They demonstrate a sense of team spirit through their interactions with others of the team.

- They are able to communicate effectively with you.

- They add different perspectives on issues without making personal attacks on you.

- They understand the need to work for the common good.

- They do what they can to make the team experience pleasant.

The Mentor

Most people who serve as mentor exhibit the following characteristics:

- They demonstrate a genuine interest in being mentors.

- They are available to assist you in any way they can.

- They challenge your beliefs with probing questions.

- They make you learn to use your own experiences to assist you in developing solutions to problems.

- They do not always give you the solutions to the problems you put before them.

- They serve in the mentor role without seeking a quid pro quo.

The Good Boss

- They demonstrate the ability to be a leader, a coach, and a referee. A really good boss does a lot of leading and coaching and become a referee only when absolutely necessary.

- They are willing to help you without giving you the answers.

- They make sure you have everything necessary to become and remain a successful member of their team, and they reward you for your efforts.

- They maintain the supervisor/subordinate relationship without appearing aloof and without making the distinction unbearable.

- They are professional and accept responsibility for managing the team.

The Good Customer

- They are generally pleasant and demonstrate a willingness to work for the common good.

- They are able to communicate effectively with you.

- They provide you with clear direction regarding their business wants and needs.

- They do not take advantage of their position.

THE BAD

The Loudmouth

- They assume they have your tacit approval to repeat anything you have said to them, even when it's been shared in confidence.

- They use Machiavellian strategies and tactics in their efforts to get ahead, or at least to not lose ground.

- They burn almost any bridge in order to avoid being labeled as the person responsible for making a mistake.

The Know-It-All

- They truly believe they are expected to know the answer to any question, even if they have to make it up.

- They rarely take the time to think before they speak.

- They exhibit no meaningful team-oriented behavior.

- They claim responsibility for any success by declaring it was their idea in the first place. They avoid any failure by saying, "It would have worked if only they'd listened to me and done it my way!"

The Drunk

- They have somewhat similar likes and dislikes to yours and can actually be fun to be around … some of the time.

- They are able to communicate effectively with you most of the time.

- They tend to look for the easy way out and the simplest solutions.

- They can be come belligerent at the drop of a hat if they have a snoot full.

- They can put your career and even your company at serious risk.

The Empty Suit

- They repeat the comments and ideas of others, representing them as original thoughts.

- They give the appearance of being fully engaged when, in fact, they are rarely even inside the ballpark.

- They do everything humanly possible to avoid risky assignments, especially when such an assignment requires them to be original.

The Fanatic

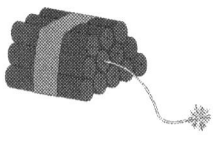

- They are very passionate and outspoken about their chosen cause or causes.

- They are unwilling and uninterested in having the opportunity to understand someone else's opinion if it doesn't agree with theirs.

- They seek revenge against those who do not conform to their definitions of right and wrong.

- They usually make disparaging remarks behind the backs of those who do not subscribe to their way of thinking.

The Spy

- They always have a hidden agenda.

- They are able to engage you in seemingly innocent conversations that are actually designed to uncover information that they will then most probably use against you, your boss, your department, or your company, depending on the circumstances.

- They can disagree with you on a topic or point without becoming belligerent in their communications style.

- They can pretend to be your friend until the spy-trap is sprung—using the information they have gathered.

- They rarely come to your aid in times of need.

The Bad Boss

- They are more interested in being a referee that in being a leader or coach.

- They are unable to communicate effectively with you.

- They are unable to disagree with you on a topic or point without becoming belligerent in their communications style.

- They are unsupportive of your needs and goals, and will seemingly avoid opportunities to help you achieve them where practical.

- They rarely come to your aid in times of need.

The Bad Customer

- They operate under the model that the customer is always right—and they really believe it.

- They seemingly go out of their way to make things twice as difficult as they really need to be.

- They avoid giving you all the pertinent facts and figures so that your efforts on their behalf always seem to fall short of their expectations.

- They go out of their way to make sure your co-workers hear how disappointed they are in your efforts on their behalf, stopping just short of asking that you be replaced.

THE UGLY

The Ugly Owner

- They always let you know who the owner is, and usually in a very unfriendly manner.

- They have a disproportionately sized chip on their shoulders representing their know-it-all opinions of themselves.

- They rarely tell you the way something should or should not be done.

- They treat you like an asset and not a fellow co-worker.

The Boss's Kid

- They believe that they are much more capable than their sires.

- They treat you like the household help.

- They remind you frequently that they are, in fact, the son or daughter of the owner, and that someday soon they will be the owner.

- They ignore the practical, logical, and often more informed opinions of others.

- They fail to remember that few of us qualify as rich kids, and they treat us as if we all have money to burn.

The Fast-Tracker

- They immediately let you know that they know someone up on high, and will only be around long enough to get their ticket punched.

- They use people and situations for the sole purpose of furthering their own careers.

- They frequently take credit when credit is not due.

- They don't respect confidences and use any information gathered to further their own careers.

- They frequently are obnoxious in their interactions with others.

- They pretend to know much more about the big picture than they actually do.

- They offer unsolicited advice on any and all subjects, never letting their lack of knowledge interfere with their willingness to provide directions.

The Hatchet Man (or Woman)

- They are completely focused on the task at hand: getting rid of someone.

- They do not identify people as people, just as a name on the list of those that are to be dealt with.

- They are not in a position to save you, since someone else has already made the decision regarding your future.

The Ugly Customer

- They truly believe the axiom that the customer is always right, no matter how wrong they really are.

- They seemingly do everything possible to make your life miserable.

- They do not come to your aid in times of need.

- They go out of their way to make you look bad in front of your supervisors.

- They cannot be trusted to tell the truth.

The Two-Faced

- They kick butt when dealing with people below them on the organization chart, and kiss butt when dealing with people above them on the organization chart.

- They have the ability to mask their seemingly split personalities.

- They actively use your own words out of context against you to further their own personal agendas.

A WORD ABOUT NONPROFITS, ASSOCIATIONS, AND ACADEMIA

If the Shoe Fits

My exposure to nonprofit organizations, associations, and the world of academia has varied over the years. Generally I would apply the same observation I apply to business: that 80 percent of the people you meet in dealing with any of these three groups will be decent. The rest will mirror the personality types covered in The Bad and The Ugly sections.

Many good people join and contribute time as well as effort to nonprofit organizations. I had the opportunity early in my career to be one of my employer's representatives in the Crusade of Mercy charity drive here in Chicago. I have also had exposure throughout my career in the sense that I participated in a number of charity events, mostly dinners and golf outings. Further, I have known a number of executives who have participated as chairpersons, committee members, and spokespersons for several different charities. And, once again, most of these people were truly interested in helping someone else achieve something that they could not achieve on their own. Unfortunately, we also find those 20 percent who are only out to achieve something for their own benefit.

All you have to do is look at the news on TV, or read the society page in the newspaper. The community is always honoring someone who helped out this charity or that charity. Many times the person being honored is the president, CEO, or chairperson of a large business. And some times one of the honorees is actually of the bad or ugly variety. In fact, some of these individuals purposefully use their "membership" in the charity to polish their image and give the appearance of being a real decent, caring member of society.

Here's an example: In one particular case, the CEO of a company was not liked by the people he managed. He ruled the public company as if it were his own, frequently ignoring the most basic tenets of decent human interaction. Few liked him, but what could anyone do? He was the boss.

He was approached to be co-chair of a local charity. He accepted, not because of some deep down, heartfelt sense of compassion, but because he would be in the public eye and it would not cost him anything—not one red cent. Nor would it cost him any real effort on his part. And in return, he got public accolades and some ancillary perks such as golf outings, opportunities to hobnob with other "movers and shakers," dinners in his honor, and his name on a plaque. His acceptance was a deliberate action based upon his opportunistic personality.

His employees did the work. His staff contributed the time and effort to organize the events, write copy for his speeches, and solicit contributions from the employees that worked for him. And when he presented the donations he did so on behalf of the people who actually contributed, but worded his presentation in such a way that he received the thanks and gratitude. He stood in the limelight, basking in the glory of public recognition. In the end, his public image was enhanced through the efforts of the employees that he treated like indentured servants.

Let's move on to the world of associations. I've been involved in several in my working career and, once again, the 80 percent/20 percent rule applies. Most of the people who work for the association actually realize that the association was formed for the betterment of the members. They are hard working and focused individuals who try to make a positive difference in the association's services on behalf of the membership.

On the other hand, we have the association employees who seem to think that the membership exists for their own personal benefit. They attempt to exert their beliefs and opinions about anything and everything regarding the future direction of the association's membership. Every personality type we reviewed in the bad and ugly categories can be found in association employee rosters.

When the head of the association is hell-bent on imposing his own agenda on the association and membership, things really get screwed up for a while. Just keep on eye open to the business section of your local newspaper. Most of the time, when the head of an association leaves to pursue personal interests, it is because the association members told him to pack up and get out—not because he was wonderful, but because he probably was some form or other of the bad or ugly personality types we reviewed.

Further, we find some real strange people in associations who become representatives of the membership companies or constituencies when they are placed on committees. In some associations, members are expected to contribute, free of charge, an employee or two who can participate on committees involved with everything from recruiting new members to selecting sites for future conventions and trade shows. Typically, most member companies view this type of temporary assignment as a developmental opportunity for some of their employees they have identified as having star potential. So, they select real go-getters who will not only contribute to the association's efforts on behalf of the membership, but will also gain personal developmental opportunities as they encounter new challenges.

Unfortunately, however, a few member companies see this as an opportunity to take some marginal employees and foist them off on the unsuspecting association. On the surface, they have helped the association by offering up an employee. Below the tip of the iceberg, all that they have really done is make a lot of other individuals unhappy because they now have to deal with Dan the drunk or Fran the fanatic.

Our last quick overview tackles the world of academia. Just think back on your own education. Some teachers were positively delightful, while others were the kiss of death. Some teachers go out of their way to help you learn while others pride themselves on never having graded on a curve. Some teachers gain personal satisfaction seeing you graduate to the next level while others delight in your failing to pass.

Look at any newspaper and you'll see some head of some university in some state getting the people upset because he wants to change this tradition or that tradition. Or someone wants to encourage a broader student base, or a more restricted student base. Or, the president wants to reduce the number of sports scholarships and increase the number of academic scholarships—or vice versa. But whatever the issue, these few extremists treat the college or university as if it were their own fiefdom and proceed to rule the roost according to their own personal agenda. Unfortunately, many of them get away with it for years while making a lot of other people frustrated in the process.

An old saw suggests that people who can, do, while people who cannot, teach. I do not agree with this completely, but a friend reminded me that the following paraphrased quotation is attributed to Henry Kissinger, an obviously highly intelligent man: *University politics are vicious precisely because the stakes are so small.*

One very large difference between the world of academia and the world of business is that of consequence. In the business world, if you make a mistake, you run the risk of something bad happening to you. It could take the form of a dressing down by your boss, a written warning in your file, a demotion, or even a termination. But, if you're a bad teacher, you can exist for years without being found out, and the only people who truly suffer the consequences are their students who are most likely being deprived of an opportunity to learn.

For clarity though, I must confess that I did like just about 80 percent of the teachers I encountered during my schooling. Now where have I heard that statistic before?

In summary, since non-profit organizations, associations, and academia are comprised of people, it is a safe assumption that the 80 percent/20 percent rule applies in these groups as well. At least it has in my personal experiences.

THE CORPORATE MAKEOVER

Adding YOU to the equation

Right and Wrong are Relative

While I was writing this book I was engaged by a client to provide his organization with an assessment of its internal policies and procedures relative to the administration of an agreement they had in place with one of their key supply chain members. The client—we'll call it Westco—was located in the Rocky Mountain area of the country and was one of the recognized leaders in the industry it served. During the time that I worked with Westco it was announced that another company in the same industry—Eastco—was acquiring Westco. Eastco also happened to be in the same business, though their primary areas of coverage were located in the Midwest and Eastern United States. Though both firms were in the same industry, providing essentially the same products and serving the same types of markets, the geographical separation between the two meant that, in most cases, they were not considered competitors.

In my dealings with the individuals in Westco, I encountered and worked with their view of the world. There were Westco policies and procedures, Westco strategies and tactics, and the Westco vision of how a business should be run. Though happenstance, I was also aware, at an arm's length distance, of the Eastco policies and procedures as well. Obviously they had their own policies and procedures, strategies and tactics, as well as the Eastco vision of how a business should be run.

I will not attempt to judge or justify either set of rules and regulations. Each had strategies that worked, as well as strategies that did not work. One really could not assign the term right or wrong to either company's approach. Each simply had its own culture, which ultimately represented the collective essence of past practices merged with their current cadre of employees. At each company the general feeling was that their way was the right way.

When the acquisition was announced, the people at Westco suddenly were labeled as people who did things the wrong way! What tipped the balance? Simple: they were the company that was acquired.

In most mergers, managers of the acquiring company fill the management positions of the new, post-merger company. Under this premise, Newco (the name of the newly merged company in our story) would be managed at the senior levels by Eastco people. These Eastco people would use their current direct reports—other Eastco managers—to manage the Westco people. Westco policies and procedures would be given the cursory once over and then probably be discarded, with Eastco policies and procedures, strategies and tactics, and the Eastco vision of how the business should be run established as the new order at Newco.

Are Eastco policies and procedures necessarily better than those of Westco? Probably not. The same applies to a comparison of their strategies and tactics, and the vision of how the business should be run. But the golden rule applies here: The guys with the gold make the rules!

In fact, it would not surprise me to see that several time periods down the road, maybe weeks, months, or even years, some Eastco managers will covertly adopt Westco policies or procedures or strategies or tactics and present them as new and exciting improvements to the Newco way of doing business. And all of a sudden, a right that became a wrong will have gone full circle to once again become a right!

So, what does this have to do with understanding the personalities of your co-workers?

You will love this answer … everything, and nothing! And discussing this concept in the context of a merger will highlight the absurdity of what can happen.

Okay, the first answer: the scenario about setting policies and procedures in our merger story has *nothing* to do with understanding the personalities of your-co-workers. We'll tackle this first, since it is the easier of the two to understand.

In most operational business situations regarding policies and procedures, there really are not any rights and wrongs. I am not talking about human resources policies where discrimination is a definite wrong and nondiscrimination is a definite right. What I am referring to are the day-to-day operational issues that might occur in a human resources department: Should employee files be maintained in alphabetical order, or by date of hire, or by employee number, or alphabetically by departmental code? In the sales department, should sales territories be assigned by geographical locations, by dollar amounts, or by the classification of customers and prospects?

So, a merger happens. The newly combined human resources department needs to decide between maintaining employee files alphabetically, the way "we" did it, and maintaining those files by date of hire, the way "they" did it. Most reasonable people would expect those who have managerial control of the human resources department to review the merits of each approach, and simply select the best way of performing the task.

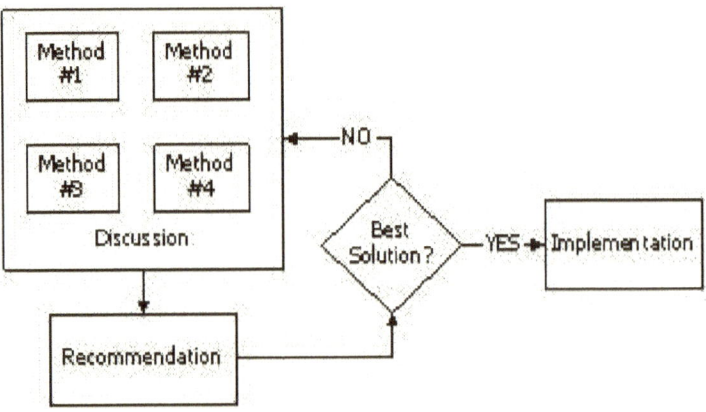

Some people in the discussion will understandably have a bias towards one system or the other, or maybe even use the opportunity to introduce a whole new system for maintaining employee files. But the fact remains that most reasonable people would expect that all approaches would be reviewed and that the best system would be selected and implemented. The same holds true for all day-to-day operational considerations. Within the limitations of computer systems, market needs, production needs, and so on, our expectation is that reasonable people will make reasonable decisions targeted to make the new organization as professional and effective as ever. You have to admit, it sounds reasonable.

You would expect participants in the discussion to have their own reasons for defending one system over another—maybe it is more efficient, requires less clerical interaction, or is more accurate. You would anticipate a reasonable level of debate as the participants try to understand each other's position so that the best method, whatever it may be, is identified and recommended as the one that should be implemented. I have participated in numerous discussions such as these and there are truly times where people are genuinely trying to identify the best of the best and can actually reach agreement on what the collective recommendation should be. While individual personalities are evident in the discussion process, the recommendation is a fact-based decision, which, though not representing the initial position of each of the participants, is an understandable decision based on the merits of those methods proposed and discussed—decisions not made on the basis of personalities, but on the basis of facts.

Now, the second answer: the scenario about setting policies and procedures in our merger story has *everything* to do with understanding the personalities of your-co-workers.

You would be surprised at how convoluted situations can become when we base decisions on those personalities and ignore a lot of pertinent facts.

Unfortunately, in many mergers, there is a winning side (the side doing the acquiring) and the losing side (those being acquired). People actually think and act this way: "Hey, we bought you. Our way of doing things must be better."

It is a rare individual on the winning side who can look at the way the losers were doing something and say, "You know, their way really is better. Let's do it that way from now on."

More often than not, the decision process becomes:

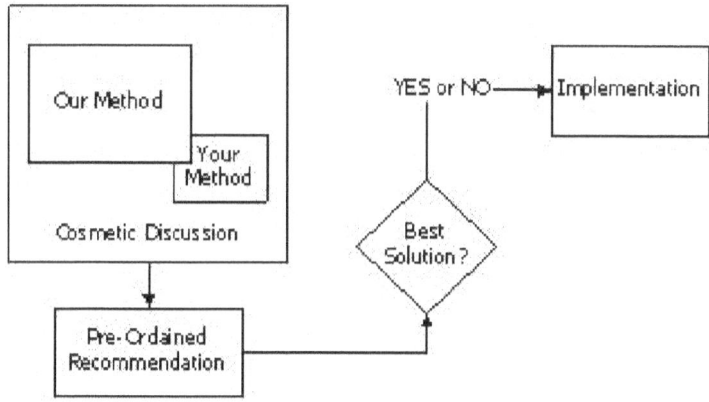

As the above model suggests, serious discussions were not intended when the task at hand was to pick the best system. A pre-ordained recommendation was a foregone conclusion to those in power.

Understanding why this happens provides insight into the character of decision makers who operate this way:

- They are insecure and need to prove to their superiors that the policies and procedures they have been following lo these many years are in fact the best: "I looked at their way and it wasn't better than our way."

- They are unable to see and understand the benefits of another way of accomplishing something because they have predetermined that a better way simply does not exist.

- They deny reality and dismiss a better idea by saying things like, "I don't believe your figures," or, "Things have changed, so your way wouldn't work anymore," or, "We just don't do things that way around here."

- They recognize a better idea, but pocket it for use later when they are pushed for a new and innovative way to improve the business. Then, all of a sudden, they have a brainstorm and, viola, and a new idea is born!

Unfortunately, many of these situations occur at such a relatively low level in the merger integration discussions that those in senior positions don't have a clue about the disservice being done to their newly formed Newco.

And these situations also happen even if not initiated by an acquisition. Other instances of this approach can be found in:

- The merger of two departments into one.

- The addition of a new boss, especially one from outside of the organization.

- The adoption of a new computer system.

- The introduction of a new line of products or services.

- The use of a new, major supplier.

- The addition of a new, major customer.

What You Might Consider Doing

In our comparisons of The Good, The Bad, and The Ugly characters, you will no doubt have noticed that the descriptions and narratives were much shorter in The Ugly section. Quite frankly, I would rather not have had to cover uglies at all, because remembering those that I have encountered along the way and using them as role models for the descriptions I wrote was taxing and discouraging. Taxing because it dragged up a lot of old memories better left buried, and discouraging because I now realize I was not savvy enough at the time of each encounter to emerge unscathed.

In any organization, the ratio of good, to bad, to ugly probably looks something like this:

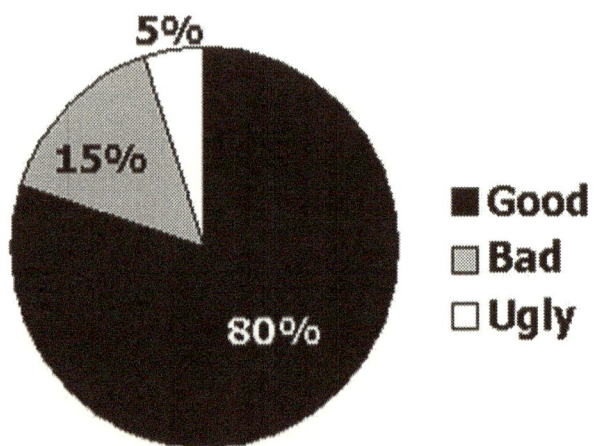

The Good: Most people you will encounter are decent. They may not become close friends but they are people you don't mind spending some time with. These co-workers are very similar to you: They have wants, needs and desires. They have responsibilities, families, mortgages, and car payments. They want to do a good job and are proud of their accomplishments.

The Bad and The Ugly: Not surprisingly, these same descriptions also apply. The difference, however, and this is an important distinction, is that they usually do not give a damn how their actions affect others, especially their co-workers. In fact, some of them will purposefully go out of their way to inflict pain needlessly. These character flaws are what you need to look out for throughout your career. You need to acquire a sixth sense about people to avoid contact with some them, and, if contact is unavoidable, to keep yourself from being affected by their destructive characteristics. And at the very least, you must minimize the damage they can do to you.

I will not be so bold as to tell you how to act. This book has attempted to present and explore some of the personality types you will encounter along the way. Each of us will find our own methods of dealing with each of the personality types. However, I will leave you with some closing thoughts as to how you can make your life and the lives of those around you a bit more meaningful and a lot more pleasant:

- Each and every day is the first day of the rest of your life. You have numerous opportunities to improve your interactions with the people you come into contact with, both on and off the job. The positive changes you make in your own approach to life have a positive impact on others. By doing something each day to improve yourself, you affect the lives of others in a positive way.

- Don't expect people to see things through your eyes, especially if it involves circumstances they have never personally encountered before. Don't rush to judge that they may not be on your side. Take the time to explain your position in a logical and calm manner and give them a chance to get on equal footing with you. Only then can you have a conversation that will be meaningful.

- If you have not fought the war, you will not understand the sacrifice. When people are very passionate about their opinions, they have their reasons. By taking the time to understand the reasons behind their passion, you will be able to better understand where they are coming from and how to continue to interact with them. Always allow someone an opportunity to save face—and, obviously, don't gloat when and if you do emerge victorious.

- You will not win every argument nor will you emerge victorious from every fight. Having these expectations will lead to frustrations, and your actions and reactions could project you as a malcontent. Many times it's better to let a decision go unmade then to force a decision that will go against you.

- Not everyone in charge is in charge because he deserves to be. Sometimes the wrong people are put in charge. Learn to deal with all types of bosses to help ensure your own peace of mind. Some people clearly should not be in charge. Just remember though, an organization might make a mistake in placing someone in charge who should not be, but that person is still in charge. Don't cut your own throat by attempting to make others aware that the current boss should not be the boss. The bad boss's own actions, or lack thereof, usually make his inability visible to all.

- You can and should make a difference in the organization in which you work. Use every opportunity to shine and use all available resources to succeed. People listen to winners and shy away from losers. Make a commitment to become and remain a winner.

- Everyone is entitled to an opinion. Rather than simply challenging their positions, get people to change their minds by presenting them with facts and perspectives that they may not have had access to.

Instead of going on and on with other platitudes and suggestions, I will end this book by saying that you, as an individual, can have a tremendous impact on your fellow co-workers. You are the only one who can decide if that impact will be positive or negative.

ABOUT THE AUTHOR

David A. Bragen is the author of the award-winning business book *A Beginner's Guide to a Successful Career* (available online at Amazon.com and Booksamillion.com) and is the founder and president of DAVEN Consulting, Inc., a firm dedicated to helping publishers make cost-effective supply chain vendor selections.

In his career, David has held a number of senior management positions with R.R. Donnelley, North American Directory Corporation, Quebecor Printing Inc., and, most recently, Quebecor World, which, at the time of his employment, was the largest commercial printer in the world. As a Division President for Quebecor World, David's responsibilities included the profit-and-loss for ten manufacturing facilities, management of a national sales force, management of a team of over 2,400 employees, and responsibility for top-line revenues of over $400,000,000.

David holds both a BBA and MBA from Loyola University in Chicago. He resides in Carol Stream, Illinois, with his wife, two children, and two dogs. He enjoys hunting, golf, woodworking, and writing.

978-0-595-40910-5
0-595-40910-5